The Energy Fields
of the Aura

Frank Lorentzen

The Energy Fields
of the Aura

Volume 1

Essencia

Copyright © Frank Lorentzen 2011
www.auric-energyfields.com
mail@auric-energyfields.com

The Energy Fields of the Aura – volume 1
First published in 2011
Copyright of this publication 2011
Original title: Auraens Energifelter
Published by Sphinx, Denmark

Translation: Klara Ivanicsova
Layout: Bente Grue
Illustrations and photography: Frank Lorentzen
Cover design: Frank Lorentzen and Bente Grue
ISBN: 978-87-994189-2-3

✻   Colour illustrations related to this book can be found at:
   www.auric-energyfields.com

All rights reserved.
No part of this book may be reproduced or utilized in any form or by any means, electronic or mechanical, including photocopying, recording, or by any information storage and retrieval system, without permission in writing from the publisher. It is permissible to quote from the book if the source is acknowledged.

Contents

- 7 Foreword

9 Chapter 1 - The Etheric Energy Field
- 10 Introduction to the etheric energy field
- 18 The seven primary chakras
- 24 The Root Chakra
- 29 The Hara Chakra
- 35 The Solar Plexus Chakra
- 40 The Heart Chakra
- 46 The Throat Chakra
- 51 The Pineal Chakra
- 56 The Crown Chakra
- 60 The twenty one secondary chakras
- 72 Important etheric points

86 Chapter 2 - Archetypal Chakra Symbols
- 87 Introduction to the energy language of consciousness
- 88 The root chakra and its archetypal symbols
- 92 The Hara Chakra and its archetypal symbols
- 97 The Solar Plexus Chakra and its archetypal symbols
- 103 The Heart Chakra and its archetypal symbols
- 107 The Throat Chakra and its archetypal symbols
- 111 The Pineal Chakra and its archetypal symbols
- 113 Dreams – Self-development – Energy field

119 Chapter 3 - The Astral Energy Field
- 119 The astral energy field
- 121 Development of the astral energy field
- 125 The higher astral energy field
- 127 The lower astral energy aura
- 130 The difference between emotions and feelings
- 134 Sympathy and antipathy
- 135 The form of the astral energy field
- 136 The astral fire
- 139 The four astral gates
- 141 Cleansing of space and aura
- 142 Astral consciousness – Astral travel – Astral projection
- 146 The astral energy field and music

147	Astral colours
148	Harmful astral colours
156	Normal astral colours
161	Higher astral colours
171	**Chapter 4 - Exercises**
172	Breathing exercises
174	Exercise with a partner
175	Grounding exercise
176	Colour visualization exercise
177	Colour meditation with the three synchronous colours
179	The honey colour
180	Special exercises
182	Overview of etheric points – front and back of the body
184	About the author
185	Music composed by Frank Lorentzen

✹ Colour illustrations related to this book can be found at:
www.auric-energyfields.com

Foreword

This book is based on my own practical experiences lasting over twenty years. The contents of this book have been thoroughly tested in everyday life and common situations it brings.

The purpose of the book is to fulfil a need for a practical and simple book that might offer its readers a deeper understanding of the concept of psychic energy or energy field in an understandable and down-to-earth manner.

At the same time, this book might offer a multilevel support to its readers to help themselves. In connection with my teaching of the book's themes, I have often been asked to transform my knowledge into a written form, while I myself, in my youth and my adulthood, missed a book of such content. In addition, naturally, my aim and wish was to share my knowledge with as many interested people as possible.

This book is addressed to everyone who has a deeper interest in the energetic aspects of the energy field. The book is divided into two volumes. This first volume deals with the etheric energy field together with its chakras and etheric points, their function, significance and location and description of the archetypal symbols associated with the human chakra system. In addition, it offers a description of the astral field (emotional body), its function and location, with detailed description of the astral colours.

What is the energy field?

The word aura means radiance. But when we want to describe the human energy system, the word "aura" is not a sufficiently wide term. The word "energy field" is a term that covers the aspects of the human energy system more accurately. The human energy field is a reflection, a mirror or a radiation of the human consciousness. This radiation of consciousness, as it expresses itself in the energy field, is best described as a subtle energy that manifests itself in different qualities. Besides the physical body, the overall energy system consists of the etheric, the astral, mental and spiritual field.

The etherical life energy

The etherical field comprises the subtle anatomy of life energy with all of its chakras, points, etherical currents, nadirs and meridians. That which is called the "bodily field" within quantum physics, also belongs to the etherical system. Etherical energy is the reason that we are alive. Therefore, knowledge of the etherical energy is very important. The etherical energy is connected to the physical body, but has a higher speed of vibration than the physical body, making it invisible but still measurable.

www.auric-energyfields.com

The emotional energy

The astral field has an even higher vibration speed and covers the entire feeling and emotional part of human nature's subtle radiance. It is the astral energy form that most people experience when they use the word energy. The vast majority of human senses, what people feel, sense and all what they associate with the energy and aura represents the elements of the astral field. Emotional energy is varied and very extensive. All the emotional states of mind affect the astral field. The atmosphere and moods of human feelings and emotions characterize the astral field; they are all experienced as colours and symbols in it. The knowledge of how these emotions and feelings affect our lives and consciousness is described and illustrated in detail.

I would like to express special thanks to Lars Muhl, Jana Lili Wermus and Marianne Mikkelsen for reading the text of this book and their language assistance, nice constructive criticism of the material, as well as for their support and inspiration.

My special thanks go to Bob Moore, Stine, Emily, Sophie and Lasse.

Finally, I would like to wish my readers a pleasant time with this book and may they find lots of inspiration in it.

> Yours sincerely,
> Frank Lorentzen

Chapter 1
The Etheric Energy Field

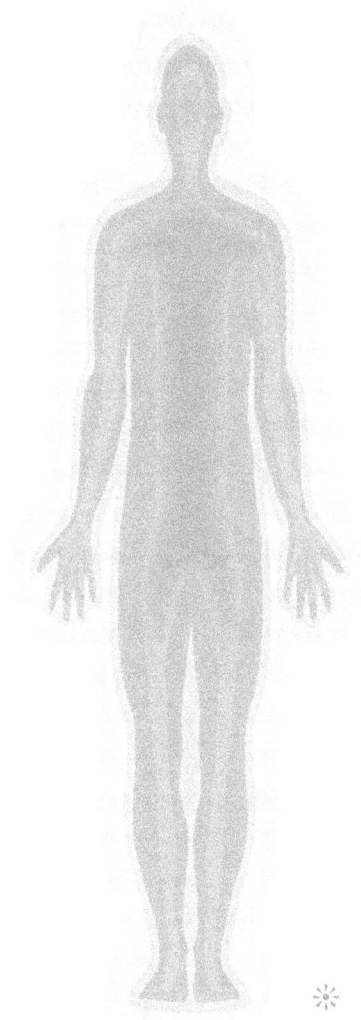

Illustration of the etheric field with the four etheric layers.

Introduction to the etheric energy field

Location in relation to the physical body
The etheric field lies closest to the physical body. It surrounds and permeates the physical body and has the same shape as the physical body. Through the aura sight it can be observed as a transparent milky white band that radiates out from the body and is approximately 10 cm thick. After the physical body, it is the most dense energy field and therefore also the most accessible source of knowledge one can have regarding a person.

History
The Eastern world has had information and knowledge about the etheric field for several thousand years. In China, the knowledge of how to strengthen the etheric field through aspects related to meridians, kinesiology and acupuncture has been present in almost everyone's life. Also, within the meditative movement form (Tai Chi) and in the treatment of symptoms and illnesses, the ancient knowledge of the etheric field has been widely used. Within the last few decades, doctors with a background in natural sciences have started to practice acupuncture in hospitals and private clinics across countries in the Western world.

Difference between the etheric field and the physical body
The difference between a dead body - 'a corpse' - and a man in a deep coma is that a person in a deep coma has got an etheric field, while a dead body does not have it any more. The etheric energy field is the life energy that keeps us alive. In the Eastern world, this vital life energy is called prana energy and chi. In the Western world, we refer to it as bioenergy and orgone energy. We human beings have an etheric energy field and it is our common feature with plants and animals. Everything that is alive has an etheric aura - without it there is no physical life as we know it.

Function
The primary functions of the etheric energy field include: receiving, storing and passing on life energy; it has a function simply to sustain life. The etheric energy field must communicate, coordinate and distribute the etheric energy into the physical body's trillions of cells so they can operate and work together as a whole. If there is any dysfunction present in the etheric energy field, we can become sick. When the body is no longer able to absorb the etheric life energy from the sun, the universe, from air and food, it dies.

The structure of the etheric energy field consisting of various chakras and etheric points

The etheric energy field is a network of energy lines, meridians, nadis and points. Where the major energy pathways intersect, there are seven primary chakras, or the 21 secondary chakras, and several etheric points that are of great importance. Besides that, there are a number of etheric points that are not mentioned nor described here, but they are utilized and very well described by other systems that work with the etheric life energy through energy pathways like acupuncture, kinesiology, shiatzu and other systems.

The four etheric layers

The etheric energy field is divided into four layers. There are two outer layers outside the body and two inner layers inside the body. The body's skin forms the natural border between the outer and inner etheric layer. The two outer layers are the health energy field and the layer of presence and manifestation. The two layers underneath the skin are called the truth layer and the layer of the inner chemical structures. The boundaries between the inner and outer layers of the etheric energy field are in constant flow, and are not so sharply delineated as in the illustration below. The purpose of this picture is simply to show the existence of the four etheric layers.

1. The health layer

The outer etheric layer outside the human body is called the health energy field and it is a reflection of everything we have inside us. At the same time, it reflects a person's health. In an average normal healthy person, it is an approximately 8 cm thick layer. When a person is healthy at all possible existing levels, the health energy field radiates.

This state of the health energy field is a desirable state that all people wish to achieve. In recent times, a growing number of people are exercising, eating healthily, not smoking - they do all this in the hope of keeping their health. It is a significantly positive fact that helps to improve public health in general. But when we look at the etheric energy field, especially at the part that reflects our health, it is not always enough to focus merely on the physical aspects such as exercise and healthy food. If you wish to achieve maximal health, there are psychological issues to be addressed and you must be able to eliminate the ones that create an obstacle in the proper flow and activity of life energy in order for the etheric energy to be able to work and act freely without any obstructions and stiffened muscles of the physical body.

2. The layer of presence and manifestation

The etheric layer just directly over the body's skin is called the layer of presence and manifestation. It is a reflection of the type of activity that has to do with our way of thinking and feeling in our everyday activities and existence and how we are able to manifest and express those inner impulses in connection with other people and life situations. This etheric layer in an average normal human being is approximately 2 cm thick. Throughout a day, a person can think and feel in incredibly varied amounts. All physical, emotional and thought-related activities characterise the layer of presence and manifestation or add colours to it.

If we find it easy to express what we feel and think, we also relatively easily manifest ourselves and act as human beings in the world that surrounds us. If we hold back our thoughts and feelings that repeat themselves over and over again and do not allow them to be expressed, it causes a hindrance in the flow of the etheric life energy and all that is reflected in the layer of presence and manifestation. In such a case, it is difficult for a person to manifest themselves as a human being. Fear of expressing certain thoughts and feelings is one of the factors that negatively influence the etheric life energy most. This is linked to the next layer, the truth layer.

3. The truth layer

The third layer that lies just under the skin is called the truth layer and it is a reflection of the authentic character of a person. It is associated with honesty, authenticity, and what is true and sincere in an individual person when he or she expresses himself or herself. This layer approximately fills half of the space inside a person's body.

The etheric energy field is always balanced in people who are honest with themselves and with their surrounding environment. There must be a reasonable correlation between who we are and what we represent as people. If we are dishonest or inauthentic (consciously or unconsciously), there is a reaction in the etheric aura, and there the truth layer is switched off.

This will cause a division and separation between the layers that are just outside the skin and just under the skin. This means the etheric energy streams that are flowing in all four etheric layers cannot function optimally, thus the entire etheric field is weakened.

All human beings have internally opposing forces and tendencies. Our feelings want one thing, the reason wants another. If we do not accept or express both truths equally, the truth layer is switched off. We exclude us from ourselves. We shut ourselves off from deeper feelings and from what is true in us and to us. We shut ourselves off from our own depths.

If we shut off our own depths, and thus shut ourselves off from the truth layer, and if such situations are present in our lives on a daily basis, we finally are unable to feel what is right. The deeper layers are not allowed to radiate out from a person's inner. The person happens to be shallow and has a split inner. The larger the inner splitting, the more split the etheric in a human being is. The free flow of energy streams in the etheric energy field is inhibited and one becomes vulnerable to diseases, etc.

The so-called lie detectors are devices that measure changes in skin moisture, whether a person speaks the truth or whether they lie. This device can measure the split between the etheric layer outside the skin and just under the skin.

If you wish to be a whole person, you must choose honesty, even if it sometimes hurts. Therefore, it often takes courage to stand alone. If you are a coward, it is better to realise it, rather than to hide it. If we feel something very deeply, it is of great importance that we express it rather than hiding it. The turquoise colour occurs in our aura when we are honest. The more the sense for honesty becomes part of our personality, the more credibility we radiate. Being honest means to show respect towards ourselves as well as towards other people.

4. The layer of the inner chemical structures

The innermost layer is called the layer of the inner chemical structures and it has a big impact on how we are able to absorb minerals, vitamins and proteins from food. It also has great importance for our ability to receive vital life energy (prana) from the sun and how we absorb it. The layer of the inner chemical structures is the etheric layer that is most associated with all vital organs, the endocrine glands and the skeletal structure of the human body.

Absorption and transformation of vital energy from the sun through the spleen point

The spleen point (also called the spleen chakra) is a double secondary chakra whose function includes absorbing the life energy from the sun's core processes. The spleen point is located at the front of the left rib edge. It is found by drawing a vertical line downwards from the left nipple to the rib edge or by drawing a horizonta line from the solar plexus towards the left rib edge. The spleen point is the main center for absorption of vital energy from the sun. This point is connected to the Solar Plexus Chakra where we hold our emotions. If a person has deep emotional problems, the function of the spleen chakra is reduced, thus the body's cells are not provided with the necessary life energy and polarity, so there is no correct voltage between positively and negatively charged energy in the cells.

If this reduction of energy takes place over a longer period of time, the cells take over a superordinate management. If this is the case, they form their own kind of polarity totally opposite to the natural complementary polarity, which can result in disorganized cell division and behaviour according to altered laws as can be observed in cases of cell changes and various forms of cancer. In cancer and cell mutations, toxins in the environment are also a decisive factor.

Absorbed life energy from the sun is distributed by the spleen point out into the whole etheric energy field, and then it is absorbed into the layer of the inner chemical structures from which the individual chakras can receive energy, depending on their function. If some chakra functions poorly, it cannot absorb as much energy as in the case of a well established function. The absorbed energy provides the chakras with streams of etheric energy that are connected to the autonomic nervous system which becomes stimulated by this process. The autonomic nervous system stimulates the hormone-producing glands and thereby the release of hormones.

1. The sun
The life-providing energy from the sun is present in the air that we breathe and in the food that we eat.

2. The spleen point
The life energy from the sun is transformed into prana energy by the double secondary chakra "the spleen point" located on the left rib edge horizontal to the solar plexus chakra.

3. Etheric streams and the seven primary chakras
The life energy then flows further through the etheric streams out to the seven main chakras and then they supply the twenty one secondary chakras and all the essential points.

4. The endocrine system
Through the transported life, energy hormones in the endocrine system are produced and this system is interconnected with the seven primary chakras.

5. Body cells
The hormones are transported through blood to trillions of cells in the body, so that they can function optimally.

How the etheric energy field is felt and seen
Many people are able to both see and feel the outer layers of the etheric energy field because it is the layer of consciousness that is easiest to see, feel and sense. If you observe a person standing against a white wall, most people doing this will be able to see the human etheric energy field. In order to see the etheric energy field, you must be relaxed. You should not focus your eyes directly on the person but look as if through the person and focus on one point a short distance behind the person. It is important to around the observed person.

If you are a sensitive person, you might perhaps feel the etheric energy field around a person through your hands. You should again be relaxed and focus your attention on your own hands. The observing person holds them at a distance of approximately

40 cm in front of him or her. Next, you should bring his / her hands slowly, in a peaceful movement, towards each other and pay attention to what happens in your hands. You may feel tingling and humming - maybe cold and warmth in them. Eventually, you may feel when his or her hands meet the etheric field of both hands. If you can feel the etheric layer of yourself, you could try to feel it in a person close to you – a friend or partner.

In this case, you should let his or her hands slowly approach the friend's or partner's physical body and be relaxed in mind when you meet the etheric energy field of that person. During this encounter, you may feel tingling in your hands when moving them towards the person's physical body. If this experience is repeated at the same place in the other person's aura again and again, you may try to sense what it is. What feeling does the observing person get? What can you see in his or her mind's eye in connection with that tingling or humming feeling in your hands? This emotional and visual information may provide the observing person with an insight into what is causing that tingling and humming in his or her hands.

The etheric energy field can be measured just like the electromagnetic field can be. This possibility is used in medicine and in many alternative systems. The etheric energy field can also be photographed. The Kirilan method is probably the best known photographic method for taking pictures of a person's etheric energetic field.

Point Consciousness

The etheric energy field contains a number of etheric points. These auric points refer to function of consciousness in a human being.

Each point in the human energetic system is associated with consciousness. When a person focuses and concentrates his or her relaxed attention on a given point in the energy field, it will trigger interference between the particular point and consciousness.

At a conscious or subconscious level, a stream of information related to condition of the particular point will begin to flow into consciousness. In order to experience this flow of information in one's inner, the person must be relaxed and calm. The flow of information can then be experienced in the form of symbols, images and moods triggered by consciousness contact with a point. By confronting this information, its significance and character, a person can see how the point and consciousness are linked.

Through this information a person can eventually help with possible imbalances. If a person does not experience internal symbols and the like, he or she should be aware of what he or she dreams about at night. In this case, the information can then be on a subconscious level, reflected in dreams. By using the energy field points, an awareness process may be going on at a much simpler level, without performing pressure on it and without crossing the personal borders.

If there is too much internal resistance in a person, he or she would lose his/her focus and concentration and slip into a stream of thoughts. Eventually, this person may fall asleep during the contact with the particular point in which unconscious material of repressed character is present.

When a person repeatedly loses his concentration and attention at certain points, we speak of blockage. The reason for these blocks only enters a person's conscious state if he or she is ready and mature enough for that kind of awareness. Should you lose attention at one point in connection with a meditative practice, you must accept it fully and return to that particular point when one becomes aware of it.

In connection with personal and spiritual development the point consciousness is of very high importance, especially if you use many points of the energy field. It is obvious that the point consciousness can be helpful in a person's development process in a truly unique way, especially if the person is mature enough for that.

The colours and location of the seven chakras in the etheric energy field

The form of energy that occurs in the seven chakras is not of etheric character, although the chakras are located in the etheric energy field. The seven primary chakras have their own colour and each colour is an expression of the consciousness contact and awareness function of a person in relation to the different chakras. At the bottom position is the red colour associated with the Root Chakra and the sacrum at the very bottom of the spine. The orange colour is associated with the lumbar vertebrae and the Hara Chakra in the middle of the abdomen, 1 to 4 finger-widths below the navel. The yellow colour is associated with the lower thoracic vertebrae and the solar plexus chakra. The green colour is associated with the upper thoracic vertebrae and the mid-chest area, where the Heart Chakra is located. The blue colour is associated with the cervical spine and the area just below the throat at the place of the Throat Chakra. The indigo colour is associated with the centre in the middle of the head where the pituitary and pineal glands can be found, as well as with the mid-forehead area, where the Pineal Chakra, about 2 cm above the eyebrows, can be located. The violet and purple colours are associated with the top of the head where the Crown Chakra, about 1 cm above the top of the skull, is located.

Etheric consciousness

A person with access to etheric consciousness has the opportunity to help people with health issues; for instance, with healing herbs, which a sick person has need of. This ability can be also helpful in combination with healing through magnetic belts or stripes and other forms of healing. Normal people fall asleep in an etheric state of consciousness. The etheric consciousness is similar to a plant's stage of consciousness. A person can achieve awareness contact with the etheric dimension, for example, through a plant, and the person can discover what this wonderful etheric consciousness is in practice. It has recently become known that plants have their own kind of consciousness. The essence of this consciousness form has been expressed in the Western world through fairy tale creatures like "fairies". In the Eastern world, fairies are called "devas". People with etheric consciousness can communicate with plant essences "elves" and "devas".

The seven primary chakras

What is a chakra?

The word "chakra" is a Sanskrit word and it means "wheel". Another name for a chakra is energy wheel. Here, in the Western world, chakras are often referred to as "energy centres". When observing a chakra from the front of the body, it looks like a spinning wheel with spokes. Due to this resemblance, it is obvious why it was given the name chakra. The number of spokes shows how many mental and spiritual functions a particular chakra has got. In the Eastern world, a chakra is often described as a lotus flower. The number of lotus petals has the same meaning as the number of spokes in a chakra.

In one way, a chakra resembles the spiral movement in whirling water when water is let out of a bathtub or sink. A chakra may also be experienced as a funnel-like energetic vortex. On the front of the body, the funnel / the chakra energetic vortex is open and four to five cm in diameter. Its funnel-like shape narrows the closer it gets to the spine, where it ends up in a point.

In a chakra, the number of spokes together with its colour indicates what kind of a chakra it is.

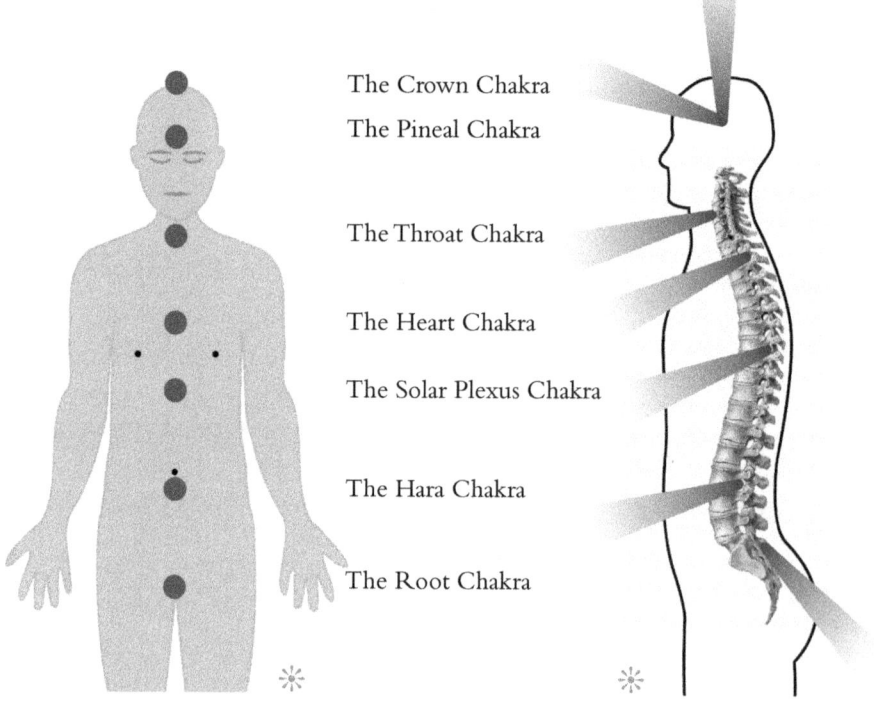

The Crown Chakra

The Pineal Chakra

The Throat Chakra

The Heart Chakra

The Solar Plexus Chakra

The Hara Chakra

The Root Chakra

For example, the Root Chakra contains four spokes, the Hara Chakra six, the Solar Plexus Chakra contains ten spokes, there are twelve of them in the Heart Chakra, the Throat Chakra has sixteen spokes, the Pineal Chakra has 96 of them and there are 998 spokes in the Crown Chakra.

The number of spokes in a chakra vortex can also be experienced as small energetic spiral-like vortexes in the chakras. If some of the small energetic vortexes of a chakra are damaged, it is a sign that one of the psychological characteristics associated with a particular chakra is damaged. If there is some deformation in one of the small energetic vortexes compared to other small energetic vortexes in a chakra, it indicates that something is not working properly in the affected chakra.

The auric relation of the chakras to various layers of the energy field can be experienced in several dimensions, depending on what the clairvoyant's consciousness chooses to tune in to. A chakra can be, for instance, experienced in the etheric energy field in multiple dimensions. The clairvoyant's consciousness can choose to tune in to the colour of a chakra, to its pulsation, rotation, or it may choose to tune in to the interior of such a chakra and even to its blockages or the small energetic vortex.

The rotating movement of the seven primary chakras in the etheric energy field i "counterclockwise", while their rotation in the astral dimension is "clockwise". In the mental dimension, the rotating movement switches back to "counterclockwise" and in the spiritual aura the rotation is "clockwise" again. These shifts in the direction of chakra rotation appear to serve as a shift of consciousness. In the physical body and the etheric energy field, the vibration of consciousness is at its lowest and can be compared with first and second gear. In the astral dimension, this vibration increases to third gear. The fourth gear in the mental system is comparable to a vibration of consciousness or its level in an everyday state of consciousness. In the spiritual dimension, the vibration of consciousness is so fast that this pace matches fifth gear.

Location

The seven primary chakras can be most clearly observed in the etheric energy field, though their energy is not of etheric character. They are also linked to the astral, mental and spiritual aura, where their energy is reflected like a glare from the chakras in the etheric energy field. The energy of the seven primary chakras is more related to the seven basic archetypal states of consciousness they represent. They are positioned like rotating energy vortexes in the energy field, where they shine with their own vibration and colour. On the front part of the body, they are located 1 to 2 cm above the skin. Their size may vary slightly from person to person, but on average the energetic vortex of each from the primary chakras on the front part of the body is about 4 to 5 cm in diameter.

Due to their shape, these energetic vortexes are like funnels that are narrowing towards the spine, where they end up in a single point that is described in detail in connection to each chakra. In these points in the back, the chakras are connected with three energy channels in the spine: Pingala, Ida and Sushumna.

Pingala (the right channel) represents the yogic, disciplined, willingness-stressed masculine development path, symbolized with a rope.

Ida (the left channel) represents the female, receptive and accepting way of development, as it is expressed in Tantra and this channel is symbolized with wings.

Sushumna (the central channel), whose path of development is symbolized by a ladder, is the individuation development path. Within western personal and spiritual development, all these three developmental ways are used.

In connection with the location of the chakras, an American doctor and specialist in radionics, Dr. David Tansley, has made a discovery. In his book, "Radionics and the Subtle Anatomy of Man", he states that in areas where the primary chakras are located, twenty one luminous energy lines are crossing each other and these twenty luminous energy lines are united in a point which is the definition of a primary chakra. As far as the secondary chakras are concerned, fourteen luminous energy lines are intercrossed and in each larger etheric point there are seven such lines intercrossed.

Accumulated energy

The energy of a chakra is an accumulation of energy that is activated at the baby's first breath. In an adult person, the energy of the various chakras is an accumulation of the energy in seven different levels of consciousness. The energy of the chakra system forms its own individual pattern because of diverse influences people are exposed to throughout their childhood and young age of adolescence. These patterns are, for example, the reason why each of us responds differently to an identical situation.

Function

Each chakra has its function and main task, which is closely associated with hormones producing glands. A chakra has two primary functions: the first function is to draw life energy in from the etheric energy field; the second is to divide and distribute this energy to, among others, the endocrine glands. Therefore, a chakra has got both physical and psychological functions that are very closely linked.

The etheric life energy, which is drawn from the etheric energy field into the chakras, is the same in all seven chakras. But it is altered when it is transmitted into the energy streams of various chakras. It becomes, so to speak, influenced or coloured by condition, function and level of consciousness of a particular chakra.

Importance of water

The human body consists of 60 percent water. Each chakra has its own pulse, sound (vibration) and colour. The pulsing in a chakra increases when we take a shower or when water evaporates from our body. This is due to the influence of water vapour on the etheric energy field. A good feeling you have after taking a bath has to do with water vapour that the etheric energy field absorbs. Water transmits energy. Water vapour that comes into contact with a chakra contains vital life energy from the etheric energy field. The stream of life energy makes the pulsation in a chakra increase. Without water vapour, the energy circulation in a chakra would be weakened.

The colour of a chakra

There are seven primary chakras, each with its own colour and each colour represents a specific awareness function. The colour of a chakra is created by its pulsation and rotation. The colour is a reflection of the consciousness state that reflects the level of consciousness and awareness function. When the colour of a chakra is clean and clear, it indicates that a chakra and its corresponding awareness function are in good condition.

Personal development and chakras

Personal development is basically an adjustment and harmonisation of the seven chakras. All chakras are equally necessary and equally positive. If a personal development process is aimed at being really successful, the seven chakras have to be in harmony with each other. Only then can a personal development process unfold in a balanced way.

In relation to the chakras this also means that one cannot favour, for instance, intellect over emotions - or spirituality over sexuality - or introversion over extroversion. In a personal development process one has to aim to achieve harmony between the different consciousness levels and chakras and in order to succeed in this it must always be related to a person's deeper nature.

It is not always easy to balance a chakra. A chakra is an energetic reflection of the consciousness function in a human being. If the awareness function is limited, superficial or it is not in line with the deeper layers of consciousness, it will be reflected in the chakra energetically. To bring a chakra back to its original pulsation and colour is a piece of developmental work that can last several years, if it is done seriously and the outcome is to be a success. If, for example, one of the small energetic vortexes in a chakra is deformed, the reason has to be resolved first. After the reason has been explained, the next step is to develop awareness of all the negative and habitual patterns of human behaviour and to stop them. When a person's negative, limiting habitual self-image in connection with the personal development process has been made conscious and integrated into personality, the affected chakra returns to its natural pulsation and colour. A deformed smaller energetic vortex will again return to its previous natural way of cooperation with other small energetic vortexes in a chakra.

A person who wishes to work with his or her chakras seriously has to devote time, commitment and not least patience to this process. There are no easy solutions in balancing a not-properly-functioning chakra, but if you are interested, you should at first be theoretically aware of the chakra system. Then you should find where some imbalances related to the chakra system can be found. You could find qualified help with a skilled therapist, healer or teacher. In order to achieve balance in chakras, there is a number of exercises at the end of this book you can do to achieve a better balance of them.

By learning about the energy field and the role of chakras, you get a clear sense of what you must develop in order to create harmony and balance. And often you get confronted with life situations that are not popular to deal with or solve, which you would like to avoid, ignore and postpone to some later time repeatedly. But it may also be some positive aspects and qualities of your personality that you have overlooked or forgotten. Every person that starts to bring balance and harmony between the chakras soon discovers the high energetic advantage of a process related to inner work on personality as a whole. Energy levels increase both in the etheric field and in the chakra system for a simple reason, that within this process you relate to the deeper nature personally. If after a few years a relatively good balance and harmony in the chakra system is achieved, the development process of a person automatically changes its direction. You automatically achieve a more intensive contact with deeper resources and qualities and thus with a greater quality of life. From a human and psychological perspective, this is a great reward.

Blockages in the chakra system

A newborn baby's chakra system is in a state of harmony and balance, even though it has been exposed to a dramatic event, to "birth". It is very rare that a child maintains this delicate form of balance in the chakra system throughout its whole childhood. All people are deeply influenced by their childhood and youth. A child quickly learns to adapt to his or her parents, and the environment, society and culture it grows up in. Acceptance and love is a necessary and fundamental need for a child to survive psychologically, but not everyone receives this. In this adaptation process, a child may have many negative experiences instead of the acceptance and love. These negative experiences are present in the chakra system as major or smaller blockages.

A blockage (in a chakra) can be observed as a dark spot inside the energetic vortex of the chakra. One of the most typical blockages, for example, is a blocked idea of a person's self image. This false self image has been implanted into a person by parents or the person's environment. Such a perception of a person's own self image is manifested as an emotional and mental behavioural pattern that is not in harmony with the person's deeper nature.

A blockage reduces pulsation and rotation in the chakra, which in turn reduces the energetic flow into the endocrine glands. This leads to a reduction of bodily functions, and thus to a reduction of energy in the health energy field.

Should you have problems with a chakra of the above-mentioned character, there are many ways to increase its rotation. When rotation is increased in a chakra, it can happen that the blockages are loosened due to heightened rotation. You can compare it with a centrifuge of the washing machine that squeezes water out of laundry. If the rotation is low, water remains in the laundry. The higher the rotation, the more water is squeezed out of the laundry. When a person begins to realize his or her original sense of self-esteem and being as such, and eventually after a period of time the person becomes aware that such state can remain stable and permanent, he or she can gradually identify with this new state of being.

One of the best known methods for increasing the rotation in a chakra is visualisation of colours. You visualise the colour that belongs to a particular chakra, feel and experience it. Then, you carefully place that colour into the chakra point, maximally for two minutes daily.

In the Hara Chakra, Solar Plexus Chakra, the Heart and Throat Chakras and in the Pineal Chakra, the colour is placed on the front part of the body. In the Root Chakra, you place the colour a bit below the sacrum, and in the Crown Chakra, the colour is placed on the top of the head.

Diseases and symptoms

In connection with a detailed description of the seven primary chakras, there is a short section on diseases and symptoms related to each chakra at the end of each description.

The Energy Fields of the Aura

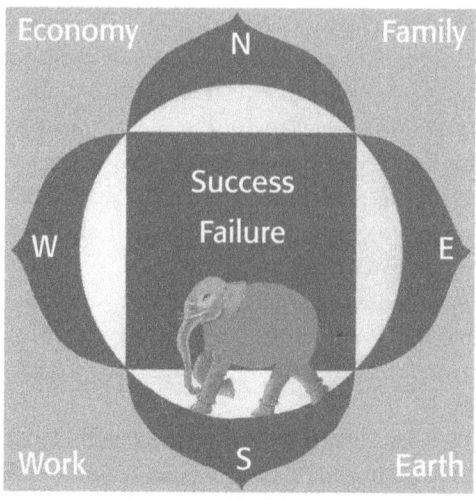

The Root Chakra

Location

At the bottom of the spine, between the coccyx and the lumbar spine, lies the sacrum. The Root Chakra (in Sanskrit it is called Muladhara) can be contacted most easily just below the sacrum. The sacrum consists of eight sacrum vertebrae fused together. A characteristic and unique aspect of the Root Chakra is that it radiates as an energy tail in the direction towards the earth from a point between the second and third sacrum vertebrae. The illustration of the Root Chakra on this page shows a lotus flower with four petals that is connected to the psychological aspect of the Root Chakra.

Root Chakra and the colour red

The red colour that is associated with the Root Chakra and the earth element is a reflection of the human consciousness function to do with physical and earth bound aspects, such as the relationship to the material world, common sense, economics, profession, family, housing, security and order in material conditions of human life. If these earth bound, physical qualities are in relative balance and stable, and there is a constant flow present, the Root Chakra is balanced.

The colour red vibrates at the lowest colour frequency of all the colours of the spectrum, but, at the same time, it is also the colour that is visible on top of the rainbow. Perhaps that is why Hindu women have a red spot on their Pineal Chakra, which stands for connection to the spiritual dimension. Personally, I have observed that small children between two and a half and up to five years are more attracted by the colour red than other colours. Perhaps it has something to do with their incarnation process into the physical world in the early years of their lives.

The colour red is also the one that creates the greatest activity in the human energy system. Therefore, you must be careful when working with red in the energy field because it can lead to overly high activity.

One of the qualities of this colour is that it brings the most original, clear and individual impulses, thoughts and feelings to consciousness, when they have not already been an integral part of a person.

The colour red brings realistic thoughts and feelings to human consciousness, so we can take a chance for action and implement what is realistically useful for us in the physical world and what we can perform in it.

Function of the Root Chakra

The physical function of the Root Chakra is connected with the excretion of an earth element. All the solid substance that the body cannot make use of are excreted through bowel movement. Plus, the Root Chakra supplies etheric life energy to feet, legs, and the adrenals.

The psychological aspect of the Root Chakra is connected with the human ability to create roots in relationships of profession, housing, economical aspects, the ability to remain realistic, practical and and to see reality as it is. The energy of the Root Chakra creates a good grounding and is associated with the ability to stand on our own two feet.

The energy in the Root Chakra is nourished from the ground and it helps us to create our own base, a starting point for our existence and that gives us a feeling of security. There is an alternative name for the Root Chakra: the security centre. This is reflected in the feeling of inner security and the ability to feel secure in ourselves, even in very stressful situations.

The ability to choose thoughts, feelings, needs and desires that cannot be realized, comes from the energy of the Root Chakra, and also the ability not to build castles in the air and not to create illusions. This gives us strength to be active and to finish projects that are realistic and useful in the physical reality. Moreover, the Root Chakra has a particularly strong connection with the Throat Chakra, communication ability and expression.

Survival instinct

The survival instinct is associated with the Root Chakra. The survival instinct sparks to life via the autonomous nervous system in extreme and life-threatening situations, such as disease, an accident and shocking experiences. Every person has a survival instinct which naturally sparks to life if there is something real to fear. When the autonomous nervous system takes over, a person can suddenly experience superhuman powers. One such example is of a mother that lifted a car which her child lay under after having been run over.

There are many people suffering from overly strong and disproportional fear of physical death, hunger and from fear of a fatal disease, which is unreal. Such a fear is tightly associated with the collective unconsciousness and with the Root, Hara and Solar Plexus Chakras.

A fear of enormous dimensions of the human energy system causes an unnecessary activation of the survival instinct that activates the adrenals and production of adrenaline and that again results in unnecessary tension and stress. In the case of persistent adrenaline production, as seen in the context of stress, it often leads to a situation in which you are not able to relax enough between physical activities. You cannot get enough rest and physical calmness.

Safety and security

Safety and security are specifically related to the Root Chakra. For everyone, it is essential to feel safe and secure. It is a basic human need. But if all our safety and security is in excess based for example on money, material benefits and symbols of personal status, such kinds of security confidence prove to be false. False safety and security is a widespread phenomenon in the Western world. A false sense of security is reflected in the fact that you choose a substitute instead of a genuine, valued product. You seek comfort in clinging to external objects. What you cannot find in yourself, you attempt to find the satisfaction and comfort in external things. One reason for this is that many people have not had the chance to have their basic security needs satisfied in their childhood. Basic security needs that have never been properly satisfied can often be traced back very far to the years of early childhood. This type of experience can be connected to the chakras as a basic experience of insecurity. Such experience of insecurity is especially connected to the Root Chakra and it is manifested as a persistent feeling of insecurity and fear and it can haunt a person throughout his or her whole life. It can manifest itself in a difficulty to stand on your own two feet. Later in life, lack of security can lead to rootlessness.

Among other things, it may manifest in greed or in strong materialistic tendencies, in overly strong career-oriented efforts or in a feeling you are worth nothing despite others seeing it differently. Everything mentioned above is an expression of the Root Chakra not unctioning well.

Importance of the Root Chakra in connection to healing

The Root Chakra has great significance in the context of a healing process. Most healing processes start as an impulse in the higher chakras, which in the ongoing development of the healing process continues to have an effect on the Root Chakra in relation to physical reality and life situation. It appears that the healing energy moves from the higher chakras down to the physical reality, where it ends. Therefore, in connection to the completion of a healing process, it is possible to observe that the healing energy on an auric basis reaches the physical basis and it connects with the ground. When the healing energy reaches the ground, final transformation and healing are present, and in the auric way, it is seen as light that rises from the ground and feet, up through the body, neck, head, and right up through the Crown Chakra and further up to the essential point that is 30 cm above the head and is integrated into all healing activities (see the second volume of the book).

Energetically, it is connected with the possibility that a person can finally eliminate negative psychological causes that once demanded attention and consciousness throughout the healing process. As soon as the healing energy reaches the ground, for the first time in the whole healing process a person is able to have a look at the real cause of his or her problems and also to accept the cause as it is, however unpleasant it may be.

You can visualise this process through a picture of pouring water (represents the problems) into a sink whose drain (connection to ground) is blocked. Water (problems) will continue to gather on the floor until the drain (ground connection) is cleaned. Only when the water finally runs out of the cleaned drains do most people first find the necessary courage to see reality with their problems, as it really is. When this happens, a person finally lets loose, and the ultimate transformation and release rise as light from the ground and upwards through the entire energy system, where everything that had been held back and repressed finally unloads through deep emotional release. It takes courage to see reality as it is, without idealisation nor projection of one kind or another. Indeed, the goal of all personal and spiritual processes is to reach the physical ground, for only there can one fully understand and appreciate the value of each healthy development.

Creating balance and positive development in the Root Chakra

The negative aspects of the Root Chakra occur when it is not in balance. Many people feel disgusted by the heaviness of this chakra. But this chakra contains a very important aspect that is connected to our vitality of the physical body each of us must be confronted with.

1. First you must recognize your imbalance in relation to the Root Chakra.
2. Then you must daily find sufficient time to provide this chakra with energy. You must be extremely disciplined, realistic and focused to follow concrete physical obligations as a human being - be it housing, finances, profession, education, physical security, physical safety, the body, food, family.
   If one or more of the above areas is not functioning as they should, you must create a realistic plan of action, preferably with help from specialists in the field and put it into practice with care and discipline. This is the most realistic way to balance the Root Chakra.

As the Root Chakra and the colour red are connected with the ground, personal development will indeed affect a person's consciousness function in connection with his or her concrete physical reality. The colour red and the Root Chakra correspond to how a person functions in his or her environment in relation to the surrounding and society. Here are some questions you can ask yourself if you are interested in whether your Root Chakra is in balance:

Are you satisfied with your social interaction with other people? – Is it easy for you to speak in a group or gathering of people? - Do you find it easy to follow projects through? - Are you satisfied with your living and working situation? - Is your economical situation satisfying? - Do you have a well organized physical life? – Does your work / profession bring you joy? – Do you have a functional social network – friends and family? - Is your relationship with your family satisfying?

If the above mentioned questions can be answered with a clear "YES", you have an excellently balanced Root Chakra. If those questions can be answered with a response that is something like "Yes, to some extent" or "Approximately so - but it might be better", you also have a relatively good contact with your Root Chakra and with the colour red. Should your answer for the majority of the questions be a "NO", you have a good piece of personal development work ahead.

Diseases and symptoms in connection with the Root Chakra

Physically, the Root Chakra affects feet, legs, and the adrenals. Some of the typical diseases and symptoms that can result from poor functioning of the root chakra is back pain in its low part – lumbar pain, varicose veins, haemorrhoids, and rectal problems.

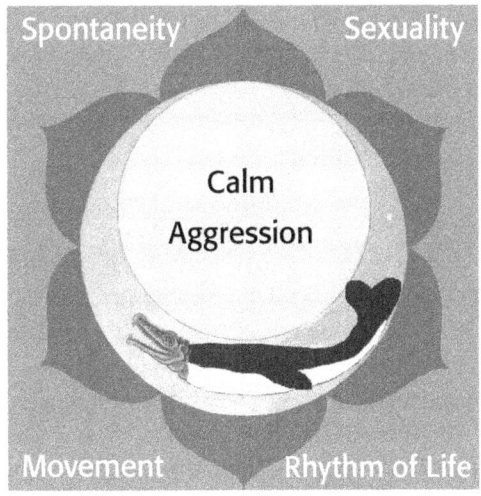

The Hara Chakra

Location

The Hara Chakra is located on the front of the body, 2 to 4 cm below the navel in the center of abdomen. The energetic vortex narrows into a funnel and ends in a point between the fourth and fifth lumbar vertebrae. Therefore, you can establish contact with the Hara Chakra and feel it on the back of the body, as already mentioned, between the fourth and fifth lumbar vertebrae.

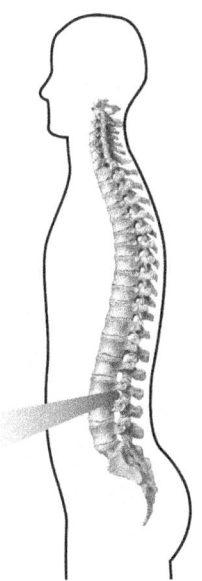

In Sanskrit, this chakra is called Svadhisthana but it is better known by its Japanese name Hara. Both Zen and karate know this chakra very well and refer to it as the gravity centre of body and soul.

The illustration of the Hara Chakra shows six petals symbolising six mental attributes associated with this particular chakra.

The Hara Chakra and the colour orange

Orange in the Hara Chakra is a reflection of a person's contact with the consciousness function related to this chakra. It has a deep impact and influence on how the etheric life energy flows in the physical body and the etheric energy field. Several aspects are attached to the colour orange. In its positive aspect it is vitalising and health building. This colour brings movement into stagnant life energy. From a spiritual perspective it gives the person a feeling of being at home in the physical world which is what is expressed through relationships, family and social relations – in fields where life energy can reach the maximum expression. From an astral / mental view, the colour orange is reflected in solid personality, healthy ambitions and well defined goals.

The positive aspect of orange also manifests itself in the Hara Chakra, when one has good and balanced contact with his or her sexuality, spontaneity and joy, when healthy instinctive impulses are not suppressed, and when there is a good contact with one's own body and with unconsciousness. Once these criteria are met, the orange colour is usually clear and pure in the Hara Chakra.

Negative aspects of the colour orange can be observed when functions mentioned above are either suppressed or exaggerated, what they often really are if certain negative, emotional states affect a person's attitudes and manners of behaviour. Then the orange will be mixed with e.g. black (unconsciousness) which creates a brownish, grey brownish colour in the etheric energy field. It is an expression of a state when life energy is stagnant and dominated by suppressed emotional tendencies.

Function of the Hara Chakra

The energetic functions and task of the Hara Chakra is to provide life energy to the physical body, especially to legs, lumbar vertebrae and the adrenals, intestines in the lower abdomen, whole pelvis and hip area, genitals, gonads and bladder.

This chakra has two basic functions: sexuality and spontaneity. The spontaneous joy belongs to the Hara Chakra. In a spontaneous person, deep, instinctive impulses and immediate incentives are easily and effortlessly expressed. There is no distortion, suppression, censoring, and calculation in a Hara Chakra-centred person. Such a person is direct and present.

The deep sexual desire impulses emanating from the Hara Chakra have for a long time represented the energy that most people have most trouble with. It is also the energy that most people are least able to handle in an authentic way. Needless to say a lot has happened in regards to public information on the collective sexual repression trend since Sigmund Freud first drew attention to it in the last century. In the case of the seven primary chakras, it is necessary that the sexual energy is associated in particular with the Heart Chakra and the Pineal Chakra, if a person wishes to achieve further personal development in this area.

Love in the Heart Chakra, consciousness and spirituality in the Pineal Chakra, together with sexual energy in the Hara Chakra creates a natural trinity in man. If a man should have maximal fulfilment of sexual orgasm, he or she must have a conscious connection to the Heart Chakra and the Pineal Chakra. If not, the orgasm is often centred in the area of genitals and legs. But if there is an existing contact to the Heart Chakra and the Pineal Chakra during sexual intercourse, the orgasm itself will expand and involve the entire etheric field. It can then expand and bring awareness into contact with spiritual energy, which brings a feeling of deep satisfaction and unity human beings find through what they are actually looking for in a sexual contact.

Many people are basically afraid of deeper sexuality, because they instinctively feel that it may open up unrecognized and often repressed emotions and memories they fear and therefore would like them rather to remain in their unconsciousness, though consciously / unconsciously they wish to have that experience. Unfortunately, it is a very common problem for many people in our sexually enlightened era. As far as deeper sexuality and its essence are concerned, there are still the same repressive mechanisms in our society as there were before.

Besides the spontaneous sexual energy, the Hara Chakra is also associated with deep rooted instinctive movements, walking, rhythm and also with its relationship to the unconscious - especially the area of unconsciousness, which Jung called the collective unconscious.

Children, who have not been shaped too much by their surroundings and environment, are aturally centred in the Hara Chakra and therefore, they act happily and spontaneously. The psychic function of the Hara Chakra is also deeply involved in the development of individuality and gender identity.

How to create balance and development in the Hara Chakra

1. First, you must recognize whether you have got problems with the Hara Chakra. Should spontaneity and sexuality not able to flow freely, you must first of all be very honest and open-minded towards yourself and towards your sexual partner. In the first step, you can benefit a lot from books which deal with the topic or from a therapist who works with sexual problems and couples.
2. The next step has to do with awareness of sexual energy. The sexual and spontaneous energy is directly related to the etheric life energy. If there are obstructions in flow of life energy, the cause mostly lies in repressed emotions.

Repressed feelings and emotions accumulate in the body and inhibit the life energy. In order to bring the stiffened and repressed sexual energy to consciousness, you can work with the body through massage forms, whose purpose is to make the stagnant life energy flow again. Again, you can find help in lots of good books, and from a possible massage teacher and body therapist in this area. When the body is relatively free from accumulated emotional energy and the etheric life energy is able to flow, naturally a connection between the Hara, the Heart Chakra and the Pineal Chakra is going to be established. It is important a person is acting through consciousness and the ability to recognise and understand, while parallel blockages of physical, etheric and psychological origin are discovered. It is important to understand that the reason for stagnant life energy often is related to unconscious thoughts, behaviour and attitudes, beliefs which must be made conscious though emotional or symbolic re–experiencing. Only through such an act will the body and the etheric system be permanently changed.
3. When a person begins to experience the energy relationship between the sexual and the spontaneous in the Hara Chakra, love in the Heart Chakra and awareness in the Pineal Chakra, he or she may begin to experience the sexual act as very deep and satisfying, perhaps for the first time in his or her life. Separation between sexuality, love and consciousness is one of the most widespread social problems of our times and it is reflected in a blooming porn industry, so-called diseases resulting from welfare, polarity diseases, rising raw violence and selfishness. If a man wishes to transcend these collective unconscious tendencies, love and consciousness must become part of the sexual.

The Hara Chakra is in relative balance when a person regularly has sexual contact with another person – in which he or she experiences passion, well being and relaxation. The sexual act will not be accompanied by a lot of activities that have a source in fantasies - he or she will rest in their sexual energy. When a person no longer suppresses his or her spontaneous and sexual impulses, and they are associated with the Heart Chakra and the Pineal Chakra, a natural control over possible self-destroying and emotional powers within the personality is achieved. Confidence in nature, environment, the spontaneous and the sexual, the unconscious, and also in graceful movements and rhythm will influence such a person.

It can be difficult to work with the Hara Chakra and its inner nature. Many people must make an extra effort in their personal development, especially regarding the one in this chakra. You can find out if your Hara Chakra is in relative balance by attempting to answer the questions below.

Do you find it easy to express yourself spontaneously? – Do you find pleasure in sexuality? – Do you feel passion? - Are you comfortable and relaxed after the sexual act?

– Do you have confidence in your surroundings and your colleagues at work?
– Do you experience joy and pleasure in your working activities? - Do you trust your inner nature? – Have you got trust in life?

If you can answer all the questions above with "YES", your Hara Chakra is in very good balance. If the questions above are answered with something similar to "somewhat so", you have a relatively well functioning Hara Chakra. If you have answered with "NO" to most of the questions, your Hara Chakra is not functioning too well. To improve the energy flow in the Hara Chakra, it is beneficial to work with breathing and body-oriented therapies.

General problems with the Hara Chakra

We live in times in which we become more and more alienated from our inner nature. At a global level this collective alienation is expressed by indifference and powerlessness towards nature or collectively repressed anger and aggression. When the UN and various governments of the world try to solve this problem, it is obvious that too many states and countries have their own large interests of a commercial and financial nature making it difficult for them to cooperate in a positively goal-oriented direction. Meanwhile, the ozone layer is still thinner, ice at the poles is melting, rain forests are still devastated in an uncontrollable way, hazardous waste materials and chemicals are still dumped at sea, dangerous genetic engineering, global pollution, death of the forests, acid rains, massive oil spill in seas and overexploitation of natural resources happen on an almost daily basis. Treating nature in this way lacks respect and is an expression of a global collective imbalance of the Hara Chakra.

Such collective imbalance of mankind in connection with the Hara Chakra is reflected in the emerging disturbances and imbalances that we can observe in our world. We see it in sperm quality in men, testicular cancer, hermaphroditic polar bears and alligators, in significant rises in skin cancer because the ozone layer is constantly getting thinner, alarming melting of ice at the poles and glaciers, ocean levels rising by two to three centimetres year by year, changes that have started to occur in global ocean circulation, global warming, etc. The reason seems to be greed and desire to control nature, and basically it means a collective fear and distrust, based on a fear of losing control and thus be dominated and controlled.

Such collective unconscious emotional force creates powerlessness and hence anger and aggression that is expressed in an uncontrolled way in the form of war. In the case of both the First and Second World War, there were large collective unconscious accumulations of aggression present in the collective human astral dimension several years before the World Wars broke out. Psychologically, war seems to serve one purpose: to ease a part of the pressure in the collective unconscious.

But the responsibility for these accumulations of aggression remains on humanity. Today most of enlightened politicians are already aware of the deeper psychological reasons why major war conflicts occur. Only by gathering the world's leading politicians on the UN's initiative allowing them to pay attention to this collective, unconscious and psychic mechanism is it possible to stop major war conflicts through such awareness.

The only positive about this development is that it inevitably leads to a greater global awareness of how deeply interdependent different countries and nations are. The catastrophe in Chernobyl followed by a leak of radioactivity touched the whole world. Devastation of rainforests has an impact on the global environment. All these negative events create greater global awareness.

Once this is acknowledged by a number of countries, states and people, a new collective and more natural development of the Hara Chakra can take place in a global sense. When man is able to work with his own inner deeper nature, he cannot fail to cooperate with external nature too.

Diseases and symptoms in connection with the Hara Chakra

The Hara Chakra provides energy to the legs, lower intestines, lumbar vertebrae, whole pelvic area, appendix, genitals, bladder, adrenal glands and gonads.

Typical diseases in these areas are problems with period, infertility, vaginal infections, ovarian cysts, tumors and cell changes in reproductive organs, impotence, prostate problems, sexually transmitted diseases, low back pain, disc prolapse, bladder and urinary tract infections.

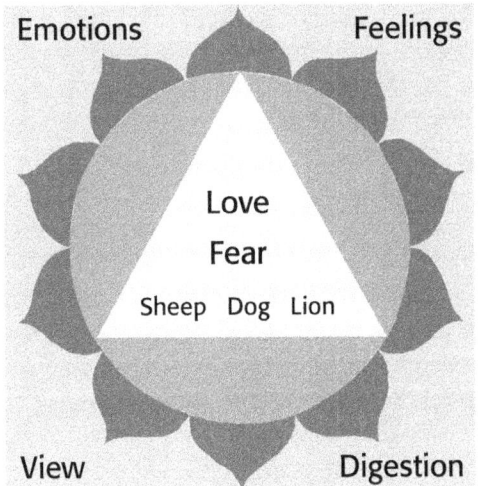

The Solar Plexus Chakra

Location

The Solar Plexus Chakra, called Manipura in Sanskrit, is located just below the ribs, a couple of finger widths below the bottom edge of the breastbone tip. The energy vortex narrows into a point between the seventh and eighth thoracic vertebrae. Therefore, the easiest way to establish contact with the Solar Plexus Chakra is on the back of the body, or in a point in the middle of the back, between the lower tips of the shoulder blades.

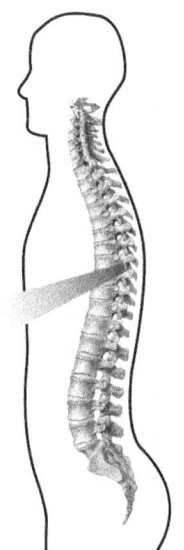

The illustration of the Solar Plexus Chakra at the top of the page shows a lotus flower with ten petals, symbolising the ten psychological characteristics of this chakra.

The colour yellow

Yellow colour in the Solar Plexus Chakra is a reflection of a person's consciousness function in relation to his or her feelings and emotions, ranging from a fiery state of being in love with someone, outbreaks of happiness, anger, all types of fears, disappointments, to sensitive and intuitive knowledge. Yellow is the colour of the sun, because it contains most light. It radiates a feeling of human warmth. This warmth comes from the inner fire and from the element of fire that relates to the Solar Plexus Chakra. Yellow has many shades that reflect our relationship to the element of fire. There are strong shades of yellow, showing our relationship to our own personal strength and outgoing nature, and there are fine, delicate yellow hues that show the relationship to our sensitive, intuitive, introspective nature. The yellow colour in a person's Solar Plexus Chakra is a mixture, a combination of stronger and finer shades of yellow. If the yellow colour in the Solar Plexus Chakra is more of a strong, bright yellow, this might indicate a personality with a perhaps overly extroverted nature. In contrast, if the yellow colour is fine and delicate, it indicates a personality of a more sensitive, intuitive nature that may be introverted. A man who has contact both with his introverted and extroverted nature, has a pure balanced yellow colour in the Solar Plexus Chakra, which is neither too strong nor too delicate.

Function of the Solar Plexus Chakra

The main physical function of this chakra has to do with degradation, digestive and absorption functions of the solid and liquid food in the stomach and intestines.

For this to happen properly, the Solar Plexus Chakra provides the vital organs with life energy. Organs as stomach, liver, kidneys, gall bladder, pancreas, spleen, digestive system and the whole middle part of the spine are concerned.

Psychical functions of the Solar Plexus Chakra: emotions

The Solar Plexus Chakra and the astral energy field (the energy field related to feelings) is the focal point of all human emotions, especially for the part of the astral energy field that is called the lower astral aura. There are positive, healthy emotions and negative types of emotions. The negative emotions are emotions in which the original emotional impulse has been distorted and clenched. The cause is an underlying fear and anxiety associated with an expression of the original emotional impulse.

This underlying fear is expressed in emotions such as selfishness, greed, jealousy, envy, rejection, hatred, fear, rage, addiction, inferiority or a sense of superiority and the like, and is usually the root cause of negative emotions. Positive emotions are characterized by the fact that they are relatively free of fear and anxiety and they are easily and effortlessly expressed. Appropriately to a situation, a person gives vent to his or her feelings and emotions. They act freely. It can be a righteous and healthy outrage, a fiery expression of anger, grief expressed by tears, spontaneous expression of joy, enthusiasm and also humour. All experiences of emotional character are related to the Solar Plexus area.

Childhood

Sympathy and antipathy are related to the Solar Plexus Chakra. From childhood, we learn what is good and what is bad. If a person should develop a balanced Solar Plexus Chakra, already from childhood he or she has to experience what confidence, self respect and belief in themself is. The child is experiencing this only through contact and a free expression of his or her emotions without fear. Children have a very open, sensitive and intuitive contact to their Solar Plexus area. If they feel there is consistency between emotions and expression in their environment, they are influenced by this consistency. So they will naturally develop a sense of self-esteem, confidence and self respect and have a natural caring for themselves and for others and a natural mental strength, warmth and energy. It is said that the astral energy field that relates to the Solar Plexus Chakra is fully developed in a young person around his or her fourteen years of age.

Self-esteem

When a person experiences that he or she is worthy of something, has self confidence and self-respect, it is because he or she has good contact with his or her emotions and expresses them easily and effortlessly. This emotional balance will be expressed through the person's reactions and deeds related to family, work, society and world. The person will be confirmed in his self-esteem from the environment and surroundings and he or she will give it back as mental strength, energy and human warmth and care.

When a person is relatively free of fear in his emotional expression, the emotional energy flows into the Heart Chakra as if by itself, where it expands from the chest area in the higher astral aura. People can experience it as warmth, compassion, joy, love, mental strength, etc. Following this, the emotion is transformed into a feeling. Emotional expression relatively freed of fear has a broadening effect on the astral energy field. Thus the astral energy field expands in a natural way. However, if there is too much fear in the expression of emotions, it has a contracting effect on the energy field. You feel emotional coldness.

Fear and anxiety

A person can associate different types of fear with different chakras, but fear and anxiety are guided by the Solar Plexus Chakra. The most dominant and most negative feeling in the Solar Plexus area is constant fear and anxiety; the real and underlying reason why healthy feelings are transformed into negative emotions. Fear can be found behind various feelings, thought and action patterns, without it being in any way obvious to people.

If a person undergoes traumatising experiences, shock, misfortune, abuse, a childhood that lacks warm feelings or severe ignorance, such experiences can sit as blocks in the Solar Plexus Chakra. The emotional blockage is an expression of fear and anxiety from certain emotions, which, when expressed, will activate a strong mental pain in the affected person.

Therefore, the person fails to express these emotions and to establish a feeling-based contact with them. This will create an internal conflict between emotional impulses and the way a person expresses himself or herself on the basis of feelings. Each time the person must express certain emotions; there is a small short circuit in his or her energy system due to anxiety and fear. This discrepancy may eventually lead to a state in which you are hardly able to feel anything; you cannot really feel happy, not really cry and laugh, do not really feel pain and love. Such a person has developed a significant fear of emotions that can evoke a large effect. A person like this will become shy in confrontation or excessively open to conflicts.

Creating balance and positive development in the Solar Plexus Chakra

1. To have a balanced relationship with your own emotions requires first and foremost that they are recognized. Emotions that are not recognized as one's own tend to create problems in life. The so-called dark sides of a person's personality are mostly unacknowledged emotions that are lying in darkness and unconsciousness and thereby they create problems of emotional character.
To recognize emotions as your own can be difficult. It is easier to identify some negative aspect in others than to recognize something of such a character in yourself. A good lesson in this: "The fact that another person triggers an emotion in my inner is evidence that the emotion is my own." Overcoming anxiety to see and recognize our own emotions is the first step in the development of the Solar Plexus Chakra.
2. The next step is to learn to be aware of your own emotions. Where can they be felt in the body? Mental massage and massage forms that aim to get the etheric life energy to flow can greatly help in this process. Emotions that are unrecognized and cannot be felt in the body tend to accumulate in the muscles and tissues. This causes the etheric life energy to be inhibited in its flow and after a period of time a good ground for physical illnesses and difficulties is formed.
3. The last step is being able to express your emotions. It is a learning process to express emotions such as anger, sadness, anxiety, helplessness, pain, worry and

fear, etc. in a balanced way. You must learn to express emotions in immediate situations that trigger them, and not later in the day, weeks or years later.

If you are not sure whether you have any problems with the Solar Plexus Chakra, here are some questions you can ask yourself. If you answer "YES" to them, you have an extremely good relationship with the Solar Plexus Chakra.

Do you find it easy to set limits, when somebody gets too close to you? Do you easily give a "YES" and a "NO" answer when it is expected from you? Do you find it easy to express emotions such as anger, grief, joy, concern and love, are you able to cry? Do you find it easy to find a balance between self-releasing and being tight-lipped in your emotional expression? Are you aware of your projections and to whom they are directed to? Do you have the willpower to say no to big temptations that you know deep down they would cross your limits and borders?

If your answers to the above-mentioned questions were reasonably moderate ones, you have a properly functioning Solar Plexus Chakra and good contact with yellow. However, if you had to say "no" to more of these questions, your Solar Plexus Chakra is not functioning optimally.

Diseases and symptoms in connection with the Solar Plexus Chakra

The Solar Plexus provides energy to the phrenic area, digestive system, gall bladder, kidneys, liver, pancreas, spleen and the central part of the spine. The most common diseases related to this body area are arthritis, stomach ulcers, gastrointestinal problems, skin problems, eczema, diabetes, inflammation and cancer of the pancreas, kidney problems, liver problems, gallstones, diseases of the adrenal glands, constipation, anorexia, bulimia, nausea and diarrhoea.

Diseases in these areas have something to do with emotions. Everyone knows the feeling in your stomach when you are affected in an emotional way or when you are nervous. As a consequence, the stomach reacts.

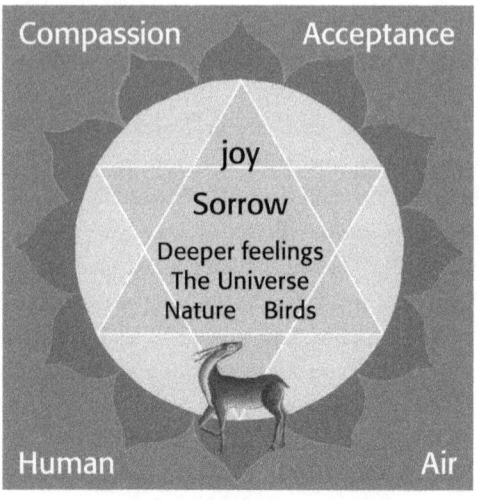

The Heart Chakra

Location

The Heart Chakra, "Anahata" in Sanskrit, has its reference point on the front of the body, in the center of the sternum. On the back of the body, the energy vortex of this chakra ends in a point between the third and second thoracic vertebrae.

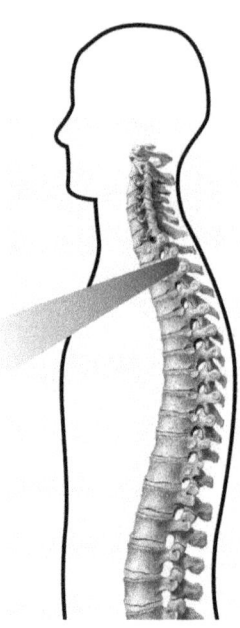

The illustration of the Heart Chakra above shows twelve lotus petals that symbolize the twelve psychological characteristics associated with this chakra. The sixfolds star symbolises the equal balance between the lower and upper chakras and the unity between the masculine active principle and the feminine passive principle. The animal with horns (here a gazelle) symbolises the rapid mental instinct and its "antenna options" (horns) refers to the higher mental character of a human being.

The colour green and the Heart Chakra

The colour green present in plants (chlorophyll) plays an important role in photosynthesis, which is part of life processes that occur in plants and enable them to absorb nutrients from soil, also water, heat and sunlight. The same ability to transform light and the creation of a green colour in the Heart Chakra is also seen in humans through their contact with earth (the Root Chakra), water (the Hara Chakra), heat (the Solar Plexus Chakra) and sunlight, which may be compared to cognitive abilities of consciousness. The light, a core condition for growth, is consciousness. Ability to transform light in connection to the three lower chakras may be compared with one's ability to grow as a person. Growth of plants and also human beings is determined by earth/soil (the Root Chakra), water (the Hara Chakra) and by heat (the Solar Plexus Chakra). If conditions for growth are not right, with too much or too little water, heat and sunlight available, it is important to provide the growth process with adequate amounts of water, heat and light that are inevitable for a successful growth process. It is a task for the consciousness – to create the right conditions for growth. Therefore, the Heart Chakra is the natural, inner center of growth, where three lower chakras and the three upper chakras can meet equally.

A really deep and lasting personal growth can only be secured when the Heart Chakra is involved. It is through the Heart Chakra that the higher part of the energy field enters the lower part of the energy field.

The green colour in the Heart Chakra is a reflection of contact with this special awareness function that comprises and naturally involves the human whole where both the high and the lower is in the area of consciousness. When this unity is present in a human, he or she has a natural access to his/her affinity with nature, the starry sky, the universe and the cosmos. Higher feelings in the form of love, compassion, humility, religion, solemnity, dignity and feeling of unity will occur naturally. All feelings of this kind are connected to the Heart Chakra.

Heart energy is deep respect, humility and love towards life itself and all its manifestations and processes. When the Heart Chakra is in balance, it will naturally result in a nice rose colour of that part of the higher astral aura, which is located approximately 30 centimetres in front of the Heart Chakra. The rose colour has an atmosphere and vibration, through which the rose horizontal heart energy flows from the balanced Heart Chakra and out into the surroundings.

When the Heart Chakra is in balance, energetically it differs a lot from the three lower chakras. If the heart energy, the rose colour, is active without any restrictions, it has a very unique characteristic: it automatically moves out in a horizontal direction and encloses other people.

Heart energy has healing properties, because this type of love is not dependent on being reciprocated. It is unconditional love. This special kind of love can also be experienced by people out in the nature or in love filled relationships with other people in who love flows freely without the motif to bind or to possess.

Function of the Heart Chakra
The Heart Chakra supplies the heart, thymus, shoulders, arms, hands, ribs, chest, breasts, oesophagus, circulatory and respiratory organs with vital energy.

Mental function
The Heart Chakra is, as it has been mentioned above, the natural balance point between the three lower and three upper chakras. High and low, good and evil, black and white are being mixed in the Heart Chakra. Contradictions in this chakra meet in the light of equality. When emotions from the Solar Plexus Chakra are no longer repressed but are penetrated by light and consciousness, they have reached a stage where they are relatively flexible and liberated in their verbal expression. When this happens in the energy system, a natural transformation of emotions occurs in the Heart Chakra, where they have a health-creating expansive effect on the entire aura. In a natural quest to become a complete human being, each person has an inner, natural transformation point. This transformation point is the Heart Chakra. Emotions into positive, outward-oriented and warm feelings are being transformed here.

Religion
In an average common person the heart energy is formed and degraded in a cycle that usually lasts seven days. Humans have always had the need to feel and to express higher feelings of the heart. One of the areas where this is expressed is in various religions. Religion and humanity are therefore inseparable. Our entire society is built on ethical basic rules or life rules that originate from religion. All natural growth processes in human life can be supported by religious life with its laws, rules and ceremonies, which are mainly involved in development and improvement of human consciousness.

Religion may also hinder a healthy personal growth, especially if religion is very judgmental and denying against impulses coming from the lower chakras. If religious persons should condemn, for example, sexual feelings or sexual impulses due to their religion, this can contribute to hypocrisy and dishonesty. It is very important that religions realize this and take responsibility for a healthy, growth supporting pedagogical approaches in connection with the lower chakras instead of demonising them. Healthy human growth cannot take place neither by suppressed nor by unilateral enjoyment of sexual and emotional impulses. Young people in all religions should be allowed to express themselves honestly about their sexual impulses and should be allowed to express strong emotions without becoming subjects to pointing fingers in a moralising and demonising way.

Individuation process and the Heart Chakra
The development of the Heart Chakra can also be performed through an individuation process. The great psychiatrist and author C.G. Jung named the superordinate human psychophysical whole as "Self" and associated its development with the Heart Chakra. Any successful individuation process will have a natural tendency to open the Heart Chakra.

Higher consciousness and the Heart Chakra
A person who is centred in the Heart Chakra has achieved a natural balance in the energy system through self-development work. This natural balance creates the basis for higher forms of energy to stream into the energy system from time to time by themselves. With this natural balance as a basis it is possible to work with higher consciousness on a conscious level. To raise awareness into light and on a higher level, meditative contemplation through prayer or meditation is necessary.

Jes Bertelsen in his book "Dreams, Chakra Symbols and Meditation" writes the following on the Heart Chakra: "This is the place where the mental mirror rotates for 180 degrees. From a viewpoint directed on the collective unconscious the view here is oriented to the higher consciousness. Control over the mental means that the personality itself can decide whether the mental mirror should reflect the earth or heaven, instinct or higher consciousness, the I or the Self. This conscious choice is achieved through meditation. Meditation means to be without thoughts, without emotions, without pictures."

Balance and self-development of the Heart Chakra
As the Heart Chakra is the natural point of balance in the human energy system, it is also the natural target for balance and personal growth. Personal development cannot happen without the Heart Chakra being involved. True personal development will never be a selfish self-indulgent endeavour. If one constantly supports the ego and self-centred goals, one has misunderstood the fundamental aspect of personal development. In a natural way, personal development involves the rest of the world, society, nature and all the people one has a deeper relationship to.

To achieve development of the Heart Chakra, a person has to train his or her ability of self-knowledge, love, compassion and self-responsibility. To understand something intellectually is different from recognising something deep in the heart. To feel love in the Heart Chakra naturally involves mental and emotional awareness simultaneously. The fusion of love between emotion and thought is a basis for compassion. Compassion involves the whole person in thoughts, words and action. Acknowledgement is often a painful, earthquake-like inner experience that involves body, mind and also spirit. Humans can be afraid of penetrating light of love and consciousness. It may be too painful to see ourselves.

Love dissolves the egoistic tendencies without ignoring the real needs of personality. Therefore, it can be hard to be centred in the Heart Chakra, before the lower three chakras are relatively developed and balanced.

The defence mechanisms that relate to the ego and the instinctual emotional impulses are related to the lower three chakras. Therefore there are only two possibilities present in this situation: "escape or confrontation". When and if they enter the unifying energy of love, they must necessarily surrender to the wholeness and love. If a person has courage and confidence to love, the defence mechanisms are dissolved. Many people feel, therefore, naked, disarmed, vulnerable and defenceless without the ego defence mechanisms, though they have no actual need of such defence mechanism in the real life situation. Putting fear and defence mechanisms aside until one actually needs them is a challenge of our deeper character and love. Initially we feel very naked and vulnerable, but slowly but surely we will find out that we are strengthened in our faith in love, in ourselves and in other people, nature, world and in earthly life.

Firstly, a person must discover his/her own wounds of soul, they must find out if there really is some need to protect themself. Then they have to start to practice how to feel love in heart on an everyday basis amid average daily routines. A person does not need to run around and show everyone his or her interests in inner love with a smiling and love filled expression in the face. They only need to share and give love to people who they believe in and think are in need of it. With such people the person is able to share it sincerely. Being in the heart is not a saviour crusade, but a deep, inner and personal matter.

The old saying "Do not throw pearls before swine" is a way to respect and honour love. You should not give your love to people who do not yet have the ability to appreciate or understand it. All of us have our own responsibility for an appreciation of love towards ourselves, towards fellow humans, nature and life.

If you are unsure whether your contact to the Heart Chakra is good, miserable or bad, you can ask yourself the following questions. If you can answer them with a "YES" you have a very well functioning Heart Chakra, and your contact with green is extraordinarily good.

Do you regularly have a deep emotional contact to either love, compassion, to the religious, transcendental, to nature and the universe? – Do you have any emotional contact with your spiritual wounds and are you aware of them? – Are you able to realise your own pain and grief? - Are you able to express your pain and grief? - Do you feel a certain kind of equality and solidarity with other people? - Do you feel joy when giving and sharing? - Do you feel this deep joy as a reward? - Do you experience clear feelings?

Diseases and symptoms in connection with the Heart Chakra

The most common defects and diseases in this region are heart attack, enlarged heart, asthma, allergies, lung problems, bronchitis, pneumonia, circulatory problems, problems in the upper part of the back and shoulders.

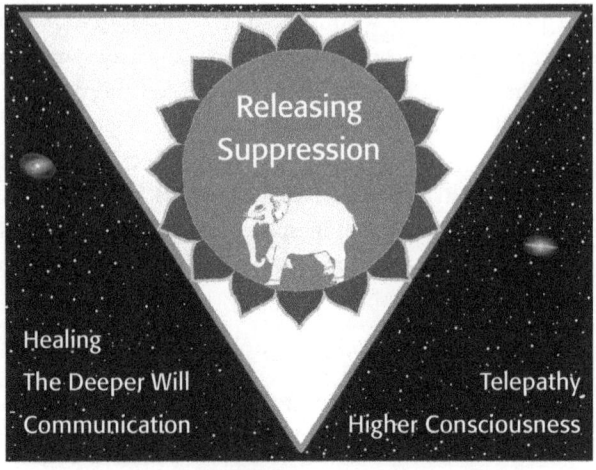

The Throat Chakra

Location

The Throat Chakra - Vishuddha in Sanskrit meaning " the pure", can be contacted best just above the hollow of the throat, and on the back of the body contact can be established at the bottom of the neck cavity between the fourth and fifth cervical vertebrae.

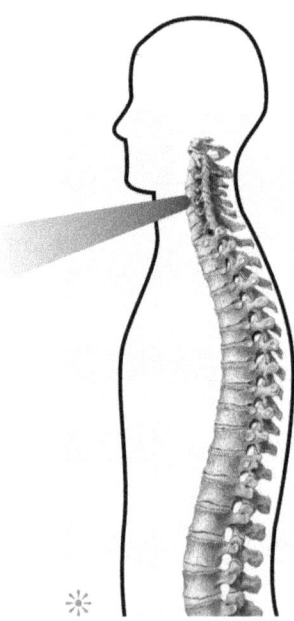

Words and terms associated with the Throat Chakra

The deeper commitment aspect, higher consciousness, the creative power, healing, communication skills, ability to be devoted, ability to concentrate, expression, release, repression, guilt complex, the colour blue – all these are words and terms associated with this chakra.

The illustration of the Throat Chakra depicts this chakra as a lotus flower with sixteen petals that symbolise mental and spiritual attributes of the Throat Chakra. The white elephant symbolises an equal relationship between physical and spiritual reality.

The colour blue

The colour blue has three aspects that are attached to it, each with its own blue shade.
1. In its extreme positive aspect, the colour is associated with higher consciousness and healing energy.
2. In its neutral element, the colour is associated with the mental energy of thoughts.
3. In its negative form, the colour blue is associated with repressing and suppressing mechanisms.

Blue (cornflower blue) is always involved in all healing situations. Emotionally it will have a redemptive effect. Mentally, it wishes to unify, create a balance and peace between the right and left brain hemispheres, between emotion and intellect.

Spiritually, it creates harmony, communication and unity between all layers of consciousness and the energy field. In neutral mental aspect this colour (dark blue) appears in the mental aura, where it shows the depth of a person's contact with his thought resources. The degree of concentration and determination in the mental system will also be reflected in connection to the neutral aspect of the blue colour.

In its negative aspect, blue (the ice blue shade) can often be observed in the energy field of people who do not express their feelings and emotions, they deny and repress them and this colour then can be observed as an ice blue shade in the lower body and in the leg area. If you have got difficulties with self expression, this is often associated with the Root Chakra as there is a particularly strong connection between the throat and the Root Chakra. Repression mechanisms are often associated with the autonomic nervous system, survival instinct and the Root Chakra, and these lie outside control of this conscious will associated with the Throat Chakra.

Function

The Throat Chakra supplies vital energy to the thyroid gland, trachea, oesophagus, cervical spine, mouth, throat, teeth, gums, jaw and ears.

The Throat Chakra has two primary mental functions that are associated with many other underlying secondary functions.
1. It is the centre of the creative force and creativity.
2. It is the centre for all communication and the ability to establish contact with other people, not only at a verbal level, but also on a musical, artistic, telepathic, mystic, spiritual and on a higher consciousness level.

The Throat Chakra is inseparably connected to human expression, sound and to human ability to listen. It determines how a person expresses himself on all levels.

The Throat Chakra is responsible for the sorting and arrangement of all internal impulses which a person allows to be expressed. Some impulses are held back and others are not. Most people know that feeling of having a lump in their throat. This happens when an impulse is held back. Often it is crying, or something a person did not express in words and it leads to the feeling of a having a lump in the throat. In such situations, the Throat Chakra reacts on suppressed impulses.

On the other hand, we can experience how redemptive energy flows when we express ourselves honestly. This positive aspect is expressed more specifically in close relationships such as marriages, relationships between partners, friendships and family relationships. But these are also areas where the greatest self-repressive tendencies are seen and experienced.

The development of higher human will, the inner voice, the ability to listen, communicate, ability to make the right decisions and the accompanying feeling of responsibility are associated with the Throat Chakra. Childhood experiences are crucial for how these fundamental human issues are developing in later stages of life. If a child does not experience the impact of both its positive and negative deeds, later it will be difficult for him or her to take responsibility for his or her own life. But if a child learns that all decisions have an impact and influence on his or her daily life and life in general, later it will be able to take responsibility for his or her life decisions more easily. A person with such experiences will be able to take and make decisions in his or her life with confidence.

The creative process is associated with creative energy of the Throat Chakra. The creative force is tightly merged with deeper and higher human will. When we say the Lord's Prayer and utter "… thy will be done, on earth as it is in heaven" it is a prayer that our higher spiritual will, deep in our heart, would be expressed in our lives. This part of the will aspect has to do with the deeper character of each person. To form your own life on the basis of deeper human will provides a person with the highest satisfaction as far as experiences as concerned. It creates the best individual life, provides you with the utmost satisfaction adjusted to deeper human needs.

A man can have many impulses in his inner. Some impulses wish to follow one direction, some a different one. When this happens, we must find a quiet place and open up to feel these different impulses. Carefully feel each impulse. How responsive is your body, mind and aura to it?

Remember: a single impulse can be an expression of a genuine deeper need and thus a reflection of deeper will. Therefore, it does not always mean that impulses from our deeper will are experienced as only pleasant. Often, the deeper will tends to confront us, to become aware and recognise attitudes that are not fully in agreement with the deeper will or with life. If the image we have of ourselves is not in accordance with our deeper will, it can be hard to see ourselves as our inners really are. If we cannot find a way towards the deeper impulses, it might be a good idea to seek help from a skilled therapist, dream interpreter or similarly skilled person.

If you are in doubt, you might try to imagine, as vividly as possible, how your life would be if a particular impulse is followed and realised. You should find the impulse that feels most right and true for you.

In connection with many contradictory impulses three rings in the Throat Chakra can be observed through auric sight. Energetically, the rings symbolise the body, mind and will of the spirit. The bigger the distance between these rings, the bigger the internal splitting in a person and the harder it will be for that person to feel his or her deeper will. The body wants one thing, the head something else and the deeper character wants also something else. When these three rings begin to be triune, or become more or less united into one ring, there is a fair correlation between the three will aspects that are associated with the Throat Chakra.

Balancing and developing the Throat Chakra

According to Freudian psychology the baby's development begins with the oral stage. The sucking reflex, and breast-feeding period are crucial for how a child develops his Throat Chakra. Should the child have negative experiences during this period, they may remain as deep mental reflexes in the person's way of expression and his/her communication ability in later in life. If the child repeatedly experiences pain and discomfort in the oral stage, this is stored as a negative experience in the whole chakra system. In particular, it is stored in the Root Chakra and in the autonomic nervous system.

If a person has fundamental anxiety associated with verbal expression and verbal communication, the affected person should be made aware of this defect in expression. Often a person needs to undergo a healing process that includes one or other form of therapy since the personal behavioural patterns that arise in connection with a fear of expressing oneself are often deeply rooted.

Next, the development should be concentrated on learning to express oneself in spoken and written form, eventually also to take rhetoric courses where you learn the art of verbal expression. This is n opportunity to practice the ability to communicate and express oneself towards the surrounding world, especially in relation to what you feel and think.

A person's self-expression is inseparably linked with the degree of the person's integration and coordination with his or her personality and deeper character. Any self-development process that is progressing well is targeted on integration of the deeper character. The greater integration there is between personality and the deeper character, the greater the transparency. Transparency means that are not any internal hidden places in the personality when a person expresses him or herself. Most inner space of the personality is recognised and made aware.

Only very few people have reached this stage. It is a life mission for all people – to dare to make a step towards agreement to accept themselves. Only by accepting yourself can you accept others. The more you are able to accept yourself and to be transparent to yourself, the more healing power is able to get through to such a person.

There are some people around the world that have reached this far. They are not always easy to find, but there is usually some form of education going on around them in which they are the teacher. They teach personal and spiritual development, meditation, religion, healing and spiritual development. One characteristic of such people is that healing energy flows freely from their inner.

These types of people very rarely appear in our lives, but such a person is naturally able to provide others with his or her free-flowing healing energy. To receive healing energy from such a person means that you have the opportunity to bring the healing energy into harmony with your own deeper personal expression.

Questions related to development of Throat Chakra

By answering the questions below you can discover if your Throat Chakra is in relative balance.

Do you find it easy to communicate with other people? - Do you easily make yourself understood? - Can you easily express what you feel, think, experience and believe? - Do you regularly provide yourself with space for your creativity? - Is your daily life without too much monotony and routine? - Do you find it easy to make a decision? Do you have good contact with your will? - Is it relatively easy for you to manifest your will and also to be honest with yourself? Do you sometimes feel the existence of a spiritual dimension?

If you can answer most of the questions with a "YES", you have a well functioning and balanced Throat Chakra. If your answer is something like "Yes, to some extent" you have a relatively balanced and well functioning Throat Chakra. If you have answered "NO" to most questions, there is some development work ahead of you.

Diseases and symptoms in connection with the Throat Chakra

Some of the most common diseases and health defects that develop in this area are pain in the throat, blisters and sore spots in the mouth, sore throat, gum problems, pain in the neck, tension headaches, swollen glands, thyroid problems, Graves' disease and goitre.

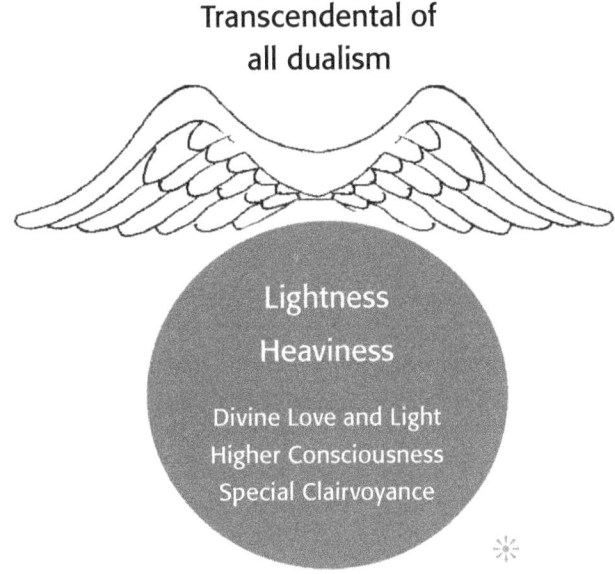

The Pineal Chakra

Location

The Pineal Chakra called "Anja" in Sanskrit can be most easily contacted in the middle of forehead, 1 to 2 cm above the eyebrows. It ends in the middle of the head in a small cavity filled with cerebrospinal fluid, where the pituitary and pineal gland is located. This point is considered to be and is called the "centre of the head."

The illustration of the Pineal Chakra at the top of the page shows two pairs of wings symbolising the final transformation of all dualistic pairs of opposites, such as light / darkness, feminine / masculine, etc. There are 96 lotus petals (they are not depicted here), and they symbolise the 96 psychological characteristics related to this chakra.

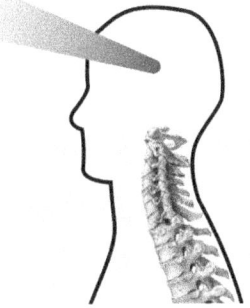

The colour indigo

The indigo colour is a dark blue-violet shade that is often seen at sea on a day with very clear and open sky, when it is sunny and windy. It is the colour associated with intelligence, understanding, intuition, intuitive feeling for the inner natural rhythm and direction of life and focusing ability. The ability to see the energy field arises from the indigo and red-violet colour vibrations that vibrate with such high frequency that it penetrates any other underlying chakra colours. This makes the ability of the consciousness to "see" oneself, other people and situations, both in a penetrating and also disturbing way. When consciousness can penetrate or be transparent to itself, it shows itself in the inner sight and phenomenon such as coloured light, garments of wise creatures and red purple flowers. When consciousness is resting for a moment and is able to reflect itself, some repressed unconscious aspects can possibly occur before the mind's eye, in the form of, for example, fluttering, rapid and uncontrollable phenomena.

When the Pineal Chakra is in balance, consciousness will rest transparently in itself, in other people and situations and that is not the case of an imbalanced Pineal Chakra.

People who are able to see clearly, who have very sharp intelligence and possess strong intuition, have good contact with the colour indigo and purple.

Function of the Pineal Chakra

This chakra provides the eyes, nose, pineal and pituitary gland with life energy for developing intelligence and a learning ability. The pineal gland (corpus pinealis – a cone-shaped part) is the only organ in the human body that has light sensitive cells.

The element of the Pineal Chakra is light. Light is the symbol of consciousness. The light of consciousness emanates from the Pineal Chakra. Our ability to "see" is determined by the presence of light and consciousness. Any experience of colour is built on the ability of the consciousness to perceive different facets and nuances. Sayings like "he saw daylight" or "to cast light on something" are describing the ability of the consciousness to "see" and to "recognise".

If a man closes the door to his consciousness, what often happens in connection with traumatic events is that the consciousness blocks the light and thus its ability to see and understand things in depth. Within psychology it is known that if a person has shut himself or herself off (and it might be a period lasting for years) from certain areas of consciousness, it tends to develop into a depression much more easily.

Daylight

Today we know that if people are not exposed to daylight throughout a longer period of time, they risk becoming depressed. Positive impact of sunlight on the mind is generally known nowadays. The light-sensitive cells in the pineal gland are stimulated and charged by sunlight (or daylight bulbs). This enables chemical signals to be led into different areas of the brain and from that place to the entire endocrine system.

Childhood

Development of inner awareness and ability to look at oneself during childhood is decisive for how the Pineal Chakra is developed. If the child's natural innate curiosity will not be impeded through negative experiences from the environment when the child inquisitively and inquiringly asks adults his or her questions again and again and if he/she gets reasonable, proper responses, he/she has a good chance to process the information in their inner. This leads to a development of ability to investigate independently and to search for answers and that is an attribute of a well functioning Pineal Chakra.

Many parents have certainly experienced that their child or children talk about colours around them or around other people or they have heard their children predicting something they could not have been aware of in any way. Many children really are able to see the energy field and sense the so-called "supernatural" things as if it were the most natural thing in the world. It is by no means something sensational or fantastic, but for them it is as natural as breathing. If you are the parents of such a child, you should listen to him or her and not reject what the child says and not consider it as pure fantasy and fabrication. Children should be listened to, not judged. They need loving and patient parents. In this way, parents provide a great service to their child or children.

If this ability is met with laughter and the children are not taken seriously, or they are scolded, or if their surroundings are scary, thenthese children block such perception or they "forget" this ability in order to meet the requirements of their surroundings in order to adapt to what is considered to be normal. In this way, already in early childhood, often a blockage in the Pineal Chakra is established. The same also applies in relation to children's eminently logical, clear thinking and questions. Children express reality as they see it, but which often leads to embarrassing feelings in their parents. If parents listen without prejudice to what their child / children say, they can discover and see the logic in children's way of thinking and inquiring. If children get reasonable answers on their very logical and often funny questions from their environment, they can also develop their Pineal Chakra more easily.

Most children lose or forget this ability by the age of seven to nine years, which is mostly connected with pre-puberty and later puberty, and it is inevitable. Learning ability and the development of intelligence is important during adolescence for the process of education.

The condition for a good learning ability is a relatively well functioning Pineal Chakra. The ability to understand, to see things in different contexts and perspectives, to think abstractly and intuitively, reflects a relatively well functioning Pineal Chakra.

Mental balance

Most adults lose some of their youth's ability for abstraction and intuitive thinking. One of the most dominant reasons for this is that our community appreciates the rational intellectual thinking much more than the irrational artistic thinking. In this way, society is losing an unbelievably great mental resource. The imbalance in priorities is generally due to a still sluggish collective progress in an understanding of the value of an equal appreciation of qualities of both brain hemispheres. In the left hemisphere, all the rational intellectual thinking is going on. The right hemisphere is the centre of all the intuitive irrational thinking. With conscious training to achieve a better balance between the brain hemispheres, the ability of an adult person to abstract and think intuitively can be restored and also a better balance can be achieved in the Pineal Chakra.

Life direction and decision-making ability

A decision-making ability corresponds with the feeling of being on the right path, of following the rhythm of life and the internal biological clock. When we have the feeling that we are following the right direction in life, it is also easier to make decisions. When we lose our sense of direction in life, we become confused and have difficulties in decision-making. The feeling of having taken the right direction arises from the Pineal Chakra. A person can very easily slip into a situation when he or she takes a series of wrong decisions and choices if they lose life direction. Hopefully, sooner or later these wrong choices lead the person back to his or her original life direction.

Today, there is a general fear of making the wrong choices. Maybe it is due to the fact that we have never had so many choices and so we are intuitively afraid to lose direction. The modern person must deal with so many things that it can be difficult to foresee the consequences of wrong choices. From this plethora of choices has arisen a need for a simpler way of life that has created a demand (fashion), in which you just try to simplify your lifestyle in all possible areas. The actual development of identity and consciousness has gone on sale and can be bought ready-made like a tailor-made spiritual candyfloss, a lifestyle with an accompanying concept. Therefore, understanding the Pineal Chakra has become more necessary today than ever before. Otherwise, people are simply seduced in one or another way. To avoid being seduced away from your life direction, it is necessary to be able to see through the seductive aspects with common sense, inner intuition and visions.

Today, a person's intuition and visions, for example through dreams or meditation, contribute to creating an inner sense of life direction. And these deep inner experiences and insights should be a basis for major decisions.

Focusing ability

The ability to focus comes from the Pineal Chakra. It is necessary to focus mental energy in order to bring structure and order into the mental system. If a person wants to make maximal use of his or her mental resources, this person must invest time to learn to focus and concentrate. Through self-discipline, focus and meditative exercises, the desired control and structure of the mental resources is achieved.

Balancing and developing the Pineal Chakra
If you are not sure whether you have a good relationship to your Pineal Chakra, you can ask yourself the questions below:

Do you find it easy to think through a problem and come up with a solution? - Do you have a good relationship with the colour indigo? - Do you have a sense of inner certainty in relation to yourself? - Do you have courage to follow this inner certainty? - Do you find it easy to concentrate? - Have you had dreams about bright, peaceful light in the form of, for example the sun, shining UFOs, shining wise creatures, shining divine people or similar? - Have you had inner, spontaneous visions in your life? - Do you find it easy to follow your intuition and be able to nuance your considerations?

If you answered with "YES" to most of the questions, you have a well functioning and balanced Pineal Chakra. If you feel you can answer "YES, to some extent" to the questions above, you have a relatively well functioning Pineal Chakra. If your answer is "NO" to several of the questions, you have a good deal of personal development work ahead.

Diseases and symptoms of the Pineal Chakra
Some of the most common diseases and problems associated with this area are brain tumors, neurological disorders, blindness, migraine, sinus inflammation, nervousness, sadness, schizophrenia and learning difficulties.

The Crown Chakra

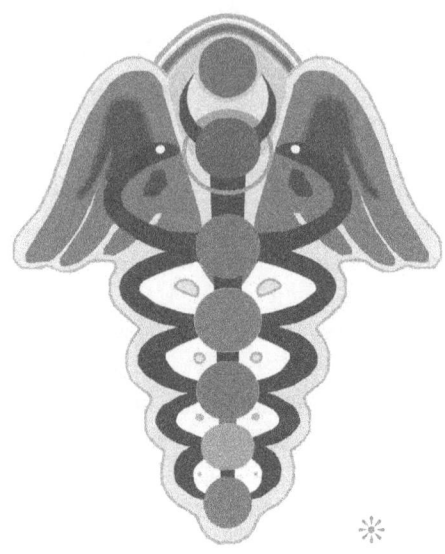

Location

The etheric upward-directed radiation from the Crown Chakra comes out from a point approximately one centimetre above the crown. The Crown Chakra is also directly connected to the centre of the head, as it is clearly shown in the illustration of its location. More subtle thought impulses from the higher mental aura are transformed

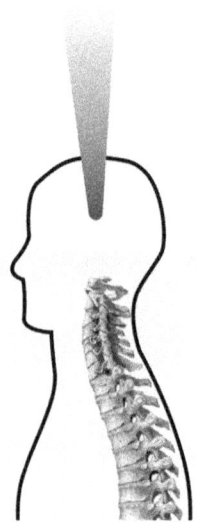

into pure thoughts in the centre of the head and they also have a direct connection to the Heart Chakra.

This chakra is called "Sahasrara" in Sanskrit. The illustration of the Crown Chakra at the top of this page shows the human skull symbolically covered with 998 lotus petals, symbolizing the corresponding 998 mental and spiritual attributes. All underlying chakras are represented in the Crown Chakra. If there is a balancing process going on in one of the underlying chakras, this activity is often reflected in the Crown Chakra in the form of the colour of that particular chakra. The top illustration depicts the Crown Chakra as a colour palette with all the colours associated with the lower chakras and also the violet Crown Chakra colour on top of the head (crown).

In a person with a relatively well balanced Crown Chakra, all chakra colours are equally present in it. When a person achieves this relative and very individual balance of the chakra system, from time to time he or she will be rewarded by the spiritual dimension in form of higher consciousness impulses. If the consciousness of such a person is developed and trained through meditation or other spiritual practices, in some years it is possible to establish a permanent contact with the higher consciousness.

The colour violet / red-violet

Of all colours that are visible to the human eye, the colour violet has the fastest frequency. When the colour frequency is increased, the colour moves into the ultra-violet colour spectrum where the human eye cannot perceive or see that colour anymore.

The German poet Johann Wolfgang von Goethe spoke of the "unseen colour" that we cannot yet perceive or see. Many people, who work with colours, call this particular shade magenta, a purple (red-violet) colour / vibration of consciousness that cannot be illustrated visually.

The high-frequency magenta is only visible to those who have the ability to see the aura. As far as this ability is concerned, it is understood as an ability to "see" and "perceive" energy in all its various forms and movements. The ability to "see" the movement of energy associated with magenta consciousness vibration is called clear-sightedness because this specific type of clairvoyance ability means to be able to "see", cause and effect in connection with all energy movements. The magenta type of clear-sightedness is like a laser sight which penetrates and encompasses another person's consciousness and unconsciousness. They "see" how cause and effect have occurred, where they are going and what the outcome will be. It is this kind of expanded higher consciousness associated with the high-frequency magenta colour vibration that reaches beyond birth and death. This awareness form is accessible to very few clairvoyant people. A person can only see this colour, if consciousness is at a higher level. Therefore, average common people do not see this colour. That does not mean that they cannot see purple shades in their daily lives. It is just not the type of purple or red-violet colour mentioned here.

Other colours

There are other colours that are also connected with the Crown Chakra. Spiritual colours like gold, silver, white or a mixture of gold and silver are associated with the Crown Chakra. Gold is the masculine spiritual nuance, while silver is the feminine spiritual nuance. When these two shades are mixed, a higher form of fusion and integration is the result and it is connected to what is called "the inner royal wedding", "the mysterious wedding" or the ultimate transformation of duality.

Function of the Crown Chakra

The Crown Chakra is a reflection of the six lower chakras, their function and balance condition and therefore it has no physical function. The function of this chakra is to create an inner feeling of wholeness, accumulation, integration and meaning. It provides continuity between the other chakras and personality aspects of a person. The better the other six chakras are cooperating, the more developed the Crown Chakra becomes and the bigger the inner experience of wholeness, coherence and meaning in life. All people are consciously or unconsciously seeking coherence, wholeness and meaning in their lives. This impulse comes from the Crown Chakra and the higher consciousness all people have an attachment to. This higher Self meditates twenty-four hours a day on personality. This alert or constantly wakeful state in humans is their higher consciousness which is expressed in inner pictures, meditation and dreams, for instance as a meditating Buddha, Christ, yogi or light above the head.

Man's spiritual dimension is thus naturally reflected in the physical world, when the other chakras are in balance. This is very important to understand when one is working with personal growth or spiritual development. It is natural to desire such a balanced and harmonious state, and it is fully possible to live an ordinary life while having a natural balance and contact with the chakra system and the spiritual dimension.

Development of the Crown Chakra

The condition of the Crown Chakra reflects the level of balance and development of the lower six chakras. The Crown Chakra is developed only through united and harmonious balanced condition of other chakras. In connection with the development of higher consciousness where the requirement to work seriously with this field is a harmonious balance throughout the whole chakra system, the daily level of consciousness is to be gradually prepared for a more intense contact with the Crown Chakra and with the higher consciousness.

Diseases and symptoms in connection with the Crown Chakra

Diseases from this area may concern the nervous system; they may be manifested in a form of paralysis, genetic disorders, bone problems and diseases such as multiple sclerosis and amyotrophic lateral sclerosis.

The twenty one secondary chakras

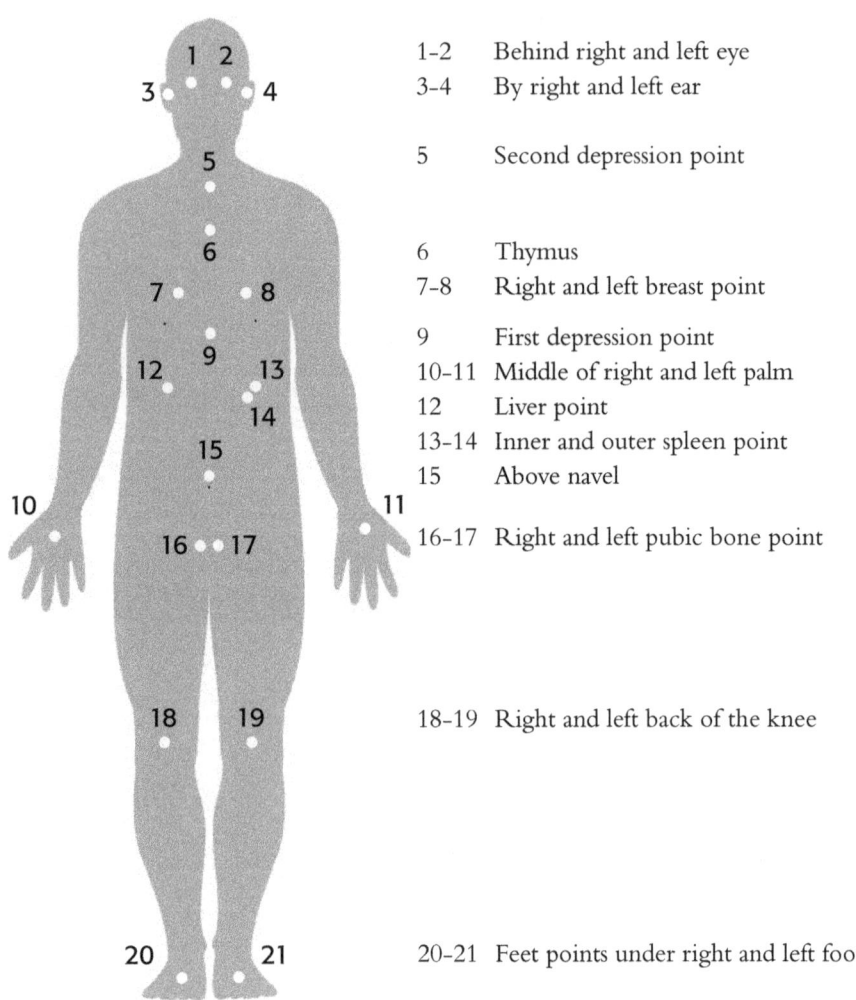

1-2	Behind right and left eye
3-4	By right and left ear
5	Second depression point
6	Thymus
7-8	Right and left breast point
9	First depression point
10-11	Middle of right and left palm
12	Liver point
13-14	Inner and outer spleen point
15	Above navel
16-17	Right and left pubic bone point
18-19	Right and left back of the knee
20-21	Feet points under right and left foot

Function of the secondary chakras

The secondary chakras are responsible for all secondary functions that are subject to the seven primary chakras. The secondary chakras are particularly associated with our five senses: sight, hearing, feeling, taste and smell; they supply the organs associated with the five senses with etheric life energy. They are also associated with our higher senses.

1-4 The secondary chakras on the head

1-2 Two secondary chakras behind right and left eye

Two secondary chakras are located behind the eyeballs of the right and left eye. Their function is to pass and maintain the supply of life energy to eyes so they can function optimally. The secondary chakras behind both eyes can be considered as transformers for the supply of life energy to the eyes.

The eyes, sight and the secondary chakras behind eyes are associated with the third eye and are supplying it with etheric life energy. Light and vision are significantly interconnected. With sight, we get the ability to see the physical reality through light. "Colours are created through encounter of light with darkness", the German scientist, artist and poet Johann Wolfgang Goethe said. "Light, shadow and colours make it possible for us to arrange the physical world through sight."

The eyes are bound by nerves with a point on the back part of the head in the area of the medulla in the brainstem where the eye nerves cross each other, so that the right eye is associated with the left hemisphere and the left eye with the right one. Balance between the right and left hemisphere characterises our vision. If a person is too much in the rational, logical left brain, he or she will predominantly make more use of the right eye. Conversely, if a person uses the right, irrational hemisphere more than the rational left one, it is reflected in the fact that they use the left eye more. It is common that a person is dominated by either the right or the left hemisphere. Most creative people are dominated by the right hemisphere, whereas most rationa people are dominated by the left hemisphere. The balanced vision, which occurs when both hemispheres are in balance with each other, is necessary for vision and brain to function properly. The reason for imbalance between brain hemispheres is mostly to be found in the function of the Solar Plexus Chakra.

If eyes should be functioning normally, meaning without glasses and other aids, primarily the Solar Plexus Chakra has to be functioning relatively well, for there should be a natural balance between hemispheres. If there are too many feelings and emotions that cannot be expressed, the repressed emotional energy is accumulated in the medulla in the top of the neck cavity. This affects and adds colour to our vision, so the world is as we see it. Your may, perhaps, never discover the emotional glasses you are wearing.

If this continues for several years, without being conscious of it, or put another way, if the Pineal Chakra cannot shine through the emotional energy so that it can become conscious, then physical eyesight starts to be affected by the accumulated emotional energy. You might need glasses or contact lenses already in your mid-twenties or early thirties, though this should only be necessary when you are about forty, forty-five years old.

Eye diseases, such as diabetes induced blindness, are an expression of a Solar Plexus Chakra which has not worked properly for many years and which is reflected in the so-called third age.

If, however, the Solar Plexus Chakra is functioning well, physical eyesight can be reduced due to age, or if a person has read too much or has stressed the eyes and sight to an exaggerated degree.

Clairvoyance and the Pineal Chakra

The Pineal Chakra, the "inner vision", is associated with the pituitary and pineal gland through the fluid-filled cavity in the centre of the head. The third eye is located right between the eyebrows, where the pituitary point is also located. To be able to use the inner vision correctly, the chakra system should be in relative balance, especially the Solar Plexus Chakra and the astral system. Otherwise, the inner vision would be influenced by too much emotional energy making it hard to see "clearly" or to have clairvoyant abilities. In this case, you cannot distinguish between what is your own energy and what is the energy that belongs to another person.

The word clairvoyance means to be "clear-sighted". The ability to see and think in a clear way may only be developed if the sight is relatively cleared of accumulated emotional energy. The more the sight is cleared from emotional impact, the clearer a person sees and the more the Pineal Chakra is involved. Should the Pineal Chakra become developed, an open and honest attitude is inevitable and it takes courage to dare to see yourself as you really are and not the way you would like to be or how others would like to see you. If you have achieved such an honest, ethical and real life attitude towards oneself and the world, then there is a real opportunity to develop the Pineal Chakra.

The ability to see aura and clairvoyance that reach out to the astral dimension is nothing spiritual in itself. Various animals also have clairvoyant abilities because of their innate instinctual astral consciousness form. This is the way a cat perceives, feels or sees if its healthy instincts are intact immediately when a person with a distinctly negative emanation enters into its field of vision. The cat immediately leaves that place. Cats and dogs can also feel astral presence in the form of people or creatures that are on an astral journey. Also, most young children under two years of age have the same ability. To spiritualise the astral dimension in your inner is related to the cleansing of the astral system, especially the emotional energy accumulated around the Pineal Chakra. At a higher conscious level each person will encounter every projection he or she carries in the inner. The more aware a person becomes about the astral dimension, the better they will be able to distinguish clearly. The ability to distinguish develops gradually, while the astral system is being spiritualised.

When working with the Pineal Chakra and with the very quick form of energy of this chakra, always bear in mind that it affects a person's entire energy system. Mental/astral stress may arise – the thyroid gland may become too active. In the case of strong useof the Pineal Chakra, the thyroid gland can become overactive. When clairvoyant persons develop these symptoms, they should take a break from their activities until their thyroid glands function normally again.

A clairvoyant can always measure the development of his vision by how far he or she can "see". In no way should this be taken as a competition, but it is a good way for a clairvoyant person to determine his or her ability to "see" clearly. The further the clear-sighted person is able to reach beyond the different layers of consciousness, the clearer and further a person with such an ability "sees". One thing is to have clairvoyant visions from the astral dimension where you can make contact with the dead, with animals, symbols and colours. Something entirely different is going on in a clairvoyant person who establishes contact with the spiritual dimension. Such spiritual contact gives access to information about cause and effect, for example, why a person has chosen to incarnate physically on a particular physical plane and on the level of direct telepathic communication with the internal supervisor; all people are associated with it in the form of spiritual advisors or "guardian angels".

Development of a clear-sighted person can be compared to different depths of perspectives. The ordinary consciousness can be compared to a man standing on the ground at the foot of a tower. On the top of the tower is another person and looks into distance. This man can be compared to a clairvoyant who has contact with the astral dimension. He shouts down to the man with general awareness that a storm is approaching on the horizon. The person with ordinary consciousness looks towards the horizon but cannot see anything because of lower visibility due to insufficient position and shouts back to the clairvoyant that he does not believe him because he cannot see anything that might indicate a storm in the distance. For the clairvoyant person who has a much wider and larger perspective than a person standing on the ground, it is not true reality. Clairvoyant persons who have contact with the spiritual dimension will have a cosmic perspective that covers the whole planet.

This picture hopefully provides the reader with a sense of depth and perspective between the astral and spiritual contact. There are quite a few clairvoyants who possess spiritual insight – or clear vision. I personally have met only two clear-sighted people who possessed such a clear vision. Both are spiritual teachers. One is Bob Moore and the other is Jes Bertelsen. Their vision permeates both the etheric, astral, mental and spiritual / cosmic dimension.

It is also common for people with clairvoyant abilities to have special access to certain areas of the energy field. For example, some are good at "seeing" into body organs, and can "see" if everything is as it should be. Others are good at feelings. They may, through their ability of "clear feeling" or sense of empathy identify what kind of feelings people are blocking or what kind of feelings are present in them. Other clairvoyants have got a natural approach to the mental aura of people who are around them and they are able to pick up on emotions, colours, thought impulses and emotional affections which may be energetically linked to emotions, chakras, secondary chakras and physical organs. When the clairvoyant ability reaches out (or in) to the spiritual dimension, consciousness has, as mentioned above, access to a cause and effect context in relation to karmic structures, but also it has access to spiritual colours and spiritual cosmic impulses.

Basically, clairvoyance is an astral phenomenon seen during the sharp scrutiny of consciousness. In relation to higher consciousness, it is about being a completely neutral observer of all kinds of impulses such as images, sensations, intuitions, colours, symbols, masters or archangels. Again, a person can measure his or her level of higher consciousness by looking at which objects the consciousness has been absorbed by, if it is "forgetting" itself and thereby falls out of its neutral observing position. If it is a beautiful colour, an archetypal symbol, an angel, a master or light that is the reason why consciousness loses its neutral position, it is because there is still something in the personality that is not finalised, something that binds consciousness to the physical plane while there is a consciousness expansion process going on in the direction of achieving higher consciousness. This higher consciousness expansion is not possible if the neutral observing consciousness gets lost in observing objects. It is, of course, a perfectly natural evolutionary process in most people who work with consciousness seriously, and it requires years of practice. But it is also extremely important to be aware of these mechanisms.

Within science and philosophy focused on higher consciousness as we see it, for instance in Tibetan Buddhism, clairvoyance is an ability humans have in common with animals and an ability all humans are born with. Clairvoyance has nothing to do with higher consciousness but the psychic ability to be spiritualised. Through work with consciousness a person can re-establish the contact with the once inborn clairvoyant ability. This usually happens when consciousness is about to penetrate the astral dimension via daily meditation. When consciousness begins to include its own astral field, it naturally also begins to include other people's astral field. When this point is reached, this ability must be cleaned so that consciousness can develop further, as the clairvoyant ability in itself is not the spiritual goal of any spiritual development. Through meditation and years of spiritual work, the clairvoyant ability can be spiritualised parallel to the spiritualisation of the astral dimension.

3-4 Secondary chakras by right and left ear

The secondary chakras in connection with the ears are situated in the middle ear. Looking directly at the face of a person, they are located inside each ear. They act as transformers for the supply of life energy, so the sense of hearing can function and be maintained optimally.

The sense of hearing

The sense of hearing, the right and left ear, are supplied with etheric life energy through the Throat Chakra. Dysfunctions in the Throat Chakra will influence the sense of hearing and even the way a person is able to listen. The sense of hearing is inextricably linked with sound elements. Through sound elements, the world gets a certain shape through language and communication. Concept formation takes place through language and communication. Sounds shape our world.

Should the sense of hearing be functioning properly, the Throat Chakra should be able to express the energy from the underlying chakras relatively easily without any repression and oppression. When you hear the expression "you hear only what you want to hear", it is an indication that only certain things are heard. The ability to listen is automatically closed. If there are impurities in the way we listen, it is usually due to suppressed emotions or unprocessed emotions. When communication involves certain emotional areas where certain repressions are present, it will automatically be closed.

The ability to listen

The ability to listen is inextricably linked with the ability to listen to ourselves. Attention focussed on ourselves goes together with the ability to pay attention to others. To be able to pay attention to ourself, a person must first process his or her repressed emotions, feelings and spiritual qualities. As they are processed, the person will discover that he or she becomes better at listening to others and to themself, too.

The expression instrument of other chakras

The sense of hearing and the Throat Chakra are expression instruments of all the other chakras. When the Throat Chakra is relatively free of impurities and expression is relatively easy and fluent, there will be an emotional contact established with what is being expressed. Thoughts and feelings are united in their expression. It is made possible by resonance. What a person says creates an automatic resonance in other people because the expression is true. Authenticity of personal expression has the greatest healing power. In Sanskrit, the Throat Chakra is called "Vishuddha" and it means "pure". When the verbal expression is pure, it is true and authentic and it creates anenormous healing ability. This healing ability is an inborn gift of all people and I call it "natural harmonic resonance." A person's integrity is expressed through the Throat Chakra.

Clear hearing

A few people come so far in their expression and listening ability that they develop the ability to hear energy. The ability to hear energy is called clear hearing. A person hears his or her inner voice and the inner voices of other people. The person can hear sounds around other people that, for example, affect them negatively in terms of stress. Negative sound may be present in the energy field even after several weeks. For example, it can be a certain sound which is present in a person's energy system and it comes from a machine at the working place that that person is exposed to several hours a day, or, it may be, for example, the sound of many loud children coming from the high noise level in a childcare centre or a kindergarten. But it may even be positive, gentle, beautiful choral music or organ music. Through certain mental techniques, it is possible to shut off the negative effects of sounds in the energy system and protect yourself in that way.

A person might be able to capture the thought frequencies another person is radiating energetically. Or a person begins to discover that he or she can establish contact with people through thoughts, telepathy, or in so-called lucid dreams, etc.

5-11 The secondary chakras in the chest area and on the hands

5   Second depression point
6   Thymus
7-8 Right and left breast point
9   First depression point
10-11 Middle of right and left palm

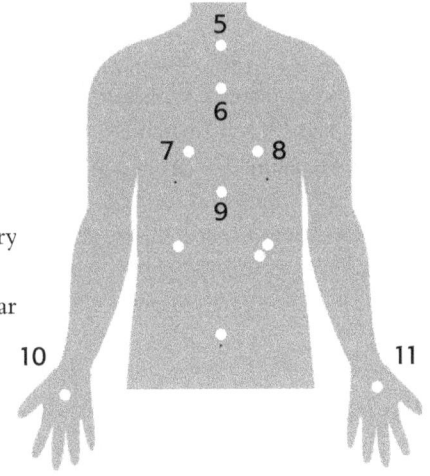

All of the seven above-mentioned secondary chakras are provided with life energy from the Heart Chakra and are connected to hear energy, sensitivity and the immune system.

5 Second depression point

Location: The second depression point can be contacted best at the upper part of the sternum just below the throat pit.

Function: When expression of heart energy through the Throat Chakra is withheld, the point becomes active in its attempts to restore the naturally outward-focussed horizontal "flow" and verbal, deep emotional expression of the heart energy. If this point is active, it also means that the heart energy is suppressed and that the state could turn into a real depression at a later time if the repression is of a continual character. There are three depression points: the third depression point is located on the chin tip, the second depression point is located on the above-mentioned body part and the first depression point is located at the bottom of sternum. They are called depression points because they all become active in the case of suppression of heart energy.

6 Thymus

Location: The thymus can be contacted most easily on the mid-chest area on the central line just below the second rib from above.

Function: This gland is associated with the immune system. When a person's self-esteem and self-confidence is good, it affects the thymus and immune function of the body in a positive way. When the above mentioned feelings are of low character, the immune system and thymus are affected negatively. In thymus protective cells are built that can fight diseases and negative health symptoms in connection with health of the physical body.

7-8 Right and left breast point

Location: The right and left breast point is located on the fourth rib edge, three to four centimetres from the central line of the body, the line where the chakras are also situated.

Function: They are associated with the natural complementary polarity structure and are connected with heart energy that flows in an outside-oriented direction. The right side is masculine and giving. The left side is feminine and receiving. The feminine heart energy is accepting and absorbing, while the masculine heart energy is invigorating, goal-oriented and precise. Try to establish contact with these points and feel where your contact is the strongest.

9 First depression point

Location: The first depression point can be found on the bottom edge of the sternum.

Function: When energy from the Solar Plexus Chakra (emotions and feelings) moves up to the Heart Chakra, it naturally flows through the first depression point. If the emotional energy and energy of feelings is hindered, limited in its flow towards the Heart Chakra, it is usually due to fears related to a person's attitude towards outer authorities based on an earlier acquired belief. If these authoritarian attitudes are not in harmony with a person's deeper individual nature, the result would be the suppression of genuine self-esteem and thus also of heart energy. When a person's heart energy is suppressed due to outer authoritarian views and opinions, the first depression point becomes active, which could indicate a problem of the above-mentioned character.

10-11 Middle of right and left palm

Location: see the illustration. The secondary chakras of both hands are located in the middle of the palm on both hands.

Function: The right and left hand are polarity points that mediate the heart energy but which also have to do with the way we express ourselves and our connection to earth. Hands are one of the areas we naturally have the most awareness of. Hands have diverse functions. With our hands, we put food into our mouths. Our ideas are transformed through our hands, for example, through crafts, art, music, writing, touch, etc. It is through our hands that our individuality is manifested physically. Therefore, hands are a significant part of our human expression, a tool through which our deeper individuality becomes apparent. Hands are a very important tool in connection with healing. It is through the secondary chakras in the middle of our palms that a healer channels healing energy.

12-15 Secondary chakras of the Solar Plexus

12　Liver point
13-14　Inner and outer spleen point
15　Above the navel

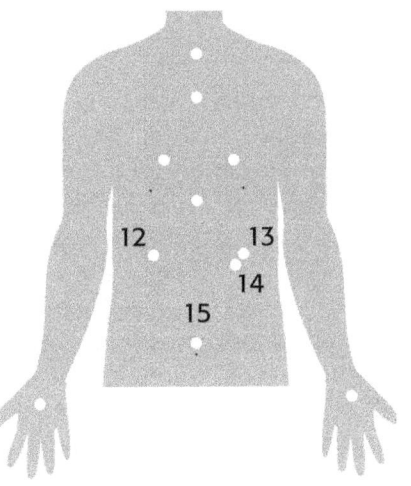

All of the mentioned secondary chakras are provided by life energy from the Solar Plexus Chakra and are to do with sight and vision. The world is as a person sees it. One of our life tasks related to personal development is to learn to see clearly. If sight is limited, it will affect the secondary chakras in the Solar Plexus, abdominal and intestinal area in a negative way.

12 Liver point

Location: This secondary chakra called the liver point is located on the right rib edge of the 7th rib, on a straight line downward from the right nipple.

Function: The liver point is very important in relation to physical and psychical health. It is also called the health point. This point together with the Solar Plexus Chakra are connected with an extremely vital energy stream that is called "the liver stream" and it is has a decisive and vital impact on our wellbeing. A negatively affected liver stream can be identified by various causes, e.g. shock, deep traumatic experiences or fear from conflicts. If the liver stream cannot flow freely, a person does not find it easy to deliver themself from something, as we say.

13-14 Spleen points

The spleen is equipped with two secondary chakras: the spleen point and the inner spleen point.

Location: The spleen point is located on the edging of the left rib edge on the 7th rib in a straight line downward from the left nipple and horizontally to left of the Solar Plexus Chakra. The inner spleen point is located on the posterior of the spleen, about five centimetres from the spleen point in the direction of the Hara Chakra, and therefore, it cannot be felt on the skin's surface. The inner spleen point is to do with internal chemical processes in the inner layer of the etheric energy field.

Function: The spleen is very important for the intake and production of etheric life energy, since it is the main centre for the intake of vital energy from the sun through what we eat, through the air we breathe, and through energy from the cosmos. If the spleen is not functioning as it should be, we get tired quickly.

15 Above the navel

Location: The secondary chakra called "above the navel" is located about 1 cm above the navel.

Function: This secondary chakra is also called the transformation point and it is also associated with the term karma. Karma can be understood as problems and challenges we meet on our way through life and it is also called regressive karma. As these challenges are being solved, the person achieves greater contact with his or her innate spiritual qualities – that is the progressive karma. When a karmic chain is eliminated, there is a transmutation of energy going on in this secondary chakra. After that, the energy can finally move towards the solar plexus and the Heart Chakra and the karmic chain is eliminated. On a personal level, the navel area is often associated with very strong emotions during birth, just after birth, and in relation to parents. All kinds of bonds, such as relationship to mother and father, have an energetic relationship with the navel area. When these strong ties begin to dissolve, withheld emotions begin to flow towards the Solar Plexus Chakra. First, they flow through the point "above the navel", where they are transformed into an emotional impulse that the affected person experiences, senses and feels. From there, the energy can flow further on towards the Solar Plexus Chakra, the Heart Chakra and the Throat Chakra, towards full acceptance and forgiveness.

16-21 Secondary chakras on abdomen, legs and feet

16-17 Right and left pubic point

Location: The secondary chakras, right and left pubic point are located at the very top edge of the pubic bone, about 2 cm to the side of the middle of this area.

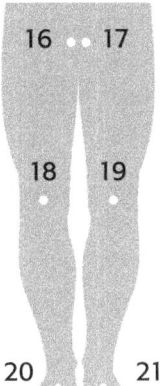

Function: These pubic points are connected to both the Root and the Hara Chakra. They are to do with a person's sexual self expression. They affect the woman's menstrual cycle, the whole emotional premenstrual period. Beside that, these points have a connection to the Throat Chakra, where they enter the natural energy connection between the Root and the Throat Chakra. A person's grounding and self-expression are important in terms of sexual orgasm. What is meant here is the kind of orgasm that involves the entire etheric field and not an orgasm which only involves the genitals. Through involvement of the entire etheric field a person's spirituality and grounding are united. In order for this to be achieved naturally, a person must have a relatively liberated expression and a good grounding in order to be able to devote himself or herself completely.

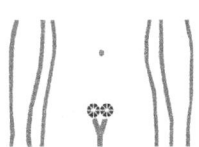

18-19 Right and left points behind the knees

Location: Both secondary chakras of the knees can be contacted most easily on the back of the knees in the middle of this area.

Function: They are supplied with energy from the Root Chakra and are related to a person's contact to his grounding. A deep red colour of the suffering aspect is often expressed in these chakras.

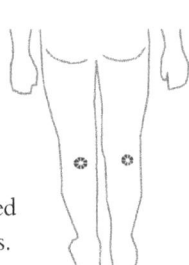

20-21 Right and left foot points

Location: The right and left foot point is located in the middle of the foot right behind the front ball of the foot.

Function: They are supplied with energy from the Root Chakra and therefore have a great significance for grounding and an inner feeling of security and success. They also are connected with the ability to find direction in life.

Important etheric points

1-18 Points around head and neck
19-30 Points around torso and arms
31-40 Points around the solar plexus, abdomen, lower abdomen and buttocks
41-48 Points around legs and feet

1-18 Etheric points around head and neck

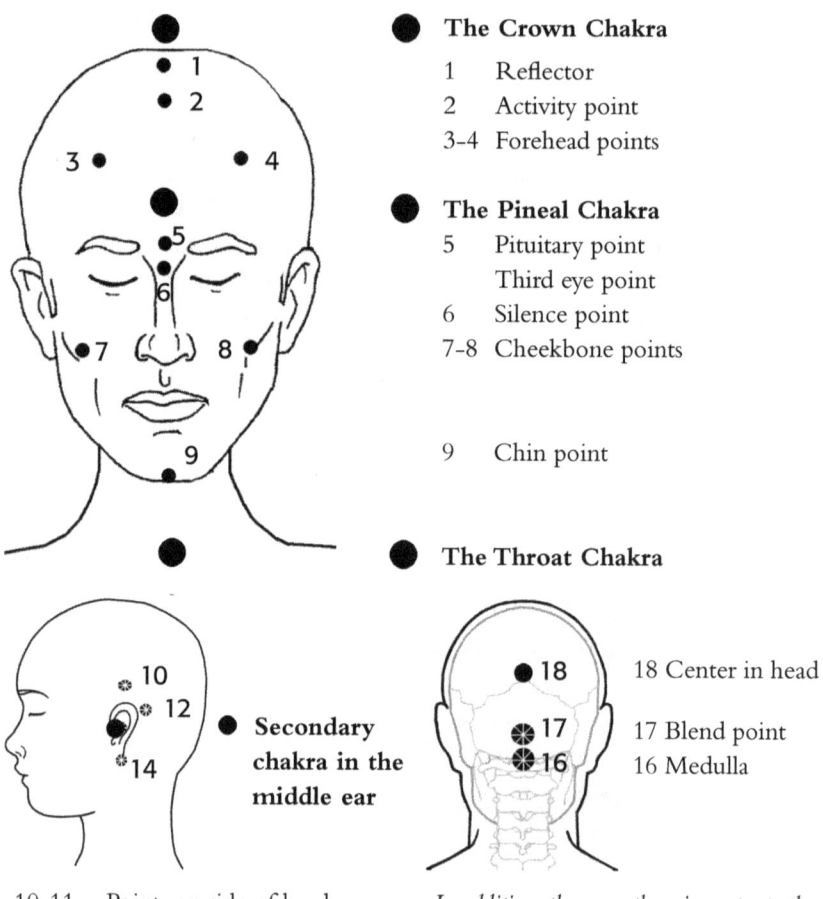

The Crown Chakra
1 Reflector
2 Activity point
3-4 Forehead points

The Pineal Chakra
5 Pituitary point
   Third eye point
6 Silence point
7-8 Cheekbone points

9 Chin point

The Throat Chakra
18 Center in head
17 Blend point
16 Medulla

10-11 Points on side of head
12-13 Awareness points
14-15 Memory points

In addition, there are three important etheric points inside the mouth and head: points that are connected with the palate (at the back of the palate), behind the front teeth and the centre of the head.

1 Reflector

Location: The reflector is located on the centre line on the upper part of the crown, on the soft spot that is open in all newborns in the first months of their lives (large fontanel). This point is located about 8 finger widths above the eyebrows.

Function: This point is to do with control over emotions and opening to a higher consciousness. The point is linked to the entire lower part of the body. If there are blockages in the lower part of the body, a person cannot achieve any proper contact with the reflector. Energetically, this point radiates upwards towards the focus point which is connected with the Crown Chakra (more detailed information will be provided in the 2nd book). The form of this energy radiation resembles the horn of the mythical creature unicorn. In addition, this point is connected to the centre of the head.

2 Activity point

Location: The activity point is located on the central line at the top of the forehead about 1 cm below the normal hairline.

Function: To establish contact with this point requires a mental balance of activity between the right and left hemisphere.

3-4 Forehead points

Location: Forehead points are located on the two "horns" on the forehead.

Function: They are also called memory points because they affect memory. They are part of the human polarity structure and they are used particularly in kinesiology to achieve balance between the two hemispheres.

5 Pituitary point

Location: The pituitary point is located midway between the eyebrows.

Function: This point has, as its name suggests, a connection to the pituitary gland inside the centre of the head. It is related to the clairvoyant ability to see auric energy. This point also has a direct connection to what, in the Eastern world, is called the third eye.

6 Silence Point

Location: The silence point is located just above the root of the nose where the forehead and nose meet.

Function: Through the silence point, it is possible to absorb sounds. In the silence point, two of the most important energy streams meet together, the negative female energy stream and the positive masculine energy stream, on their way to the Pineal Chakra. It is also a meeting point of the higher and lower mental aura on the front part of head. Moreover, both the lower and higher astral aura meet together in the silence point.

7-8 Cheekbone points

Location: The cheekbone points are located on the edge of the cheekbones.

Function: These points are to do with the energy of the head and of the Pineal Chakra. The energy of these points is particularly sensitive to stress. Therefore, they are also called the stress points. Long-term mental stress has to be taken seriously because after a longer period of time it can manifest itself in the form of multiple psychosomatic symptoms that end up in a breakdown (burn out syndrome) if stress impulses are not reduced. Stress is an expression of a unilateral influence on the energy system, where natural complementary polarity is consciously or unconsciously exceeded. This is in particular the unilateral abuse of the male, rational, logical left hemisphere, which exceeds the natural complementary polarity boundaries. A natural balancing influence of the right hemisphere is being excluded from the natural cooperation between both brain hemispheres and causes mental stress. The cheekbone points are particularly sensitive to this kind of mental stress. Mental stress can often be observed as a grey, dark green, matted lifeless shade in the lower mental field of the etheric layer and around the above mentioned points. However, stress may occur anywhere on face.

9 Chin point

Location: At the tip of the chin.

Function: The etheric point of the tip of the chin is the uppermost of the three depression points that are affected when the heart energy cannot circulate properly. They are also affected by depression, by self-pity and stress.

Etheric points in mouth and palate

At the back of the palate
Behind the front teeth (on the upper jaw)

There are two important etheric points inside the mouth that are connected to the great feminine etheric stream. One of these points is called "at the back of the palate" and it is located at the very back of the upper palate. You can bend the tongue as much as possible and thus establish a physical contact with this point. The second important etheric point in the oral cavity is located just behind the upper two front teeth in the mouth and is called "behind the front teeth". Again, you can use your tongue to make physical contact with this point. It is located between the gums and teeth.

10-15 Etheric points on right and left side of head

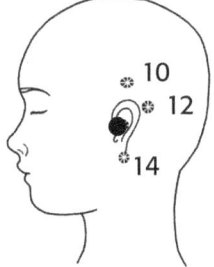

10-11 Points on side of the head
12-13 Awareness points
14-15 Memory points

● Secondary chakra in the middle ear

10-11 Points on side of the head

Location: These side points on the head are located about 2 cm above the ears.

Function: The points are connected with the etheric stream in the mental aura and the "centre of the head". They respond to physical and mental stress and mental pain (painful and torturing, repressed, unexpressed and often unconscious thoughts). They are connected with our attitude to faith and have contact with the nerve junction between the two hemispheres.

12-13 Awareness points

Location: The awareness points are located on the upper bony prominence behind the ears, about 1 cm under the upper edge of the ears on the rear in a horizontal line.

Function: They are associated, as their name suggests, with alertness, with presence in awareness in connection with the polarity structure in the mental aura, especially in relation to sound. The higher mental and lower mental aura also meet in these points.

14-15 Memory Points

Location: Memory points behind the ears are located on the bony prominence in the small hollow area behind the earlobes.

Function: These points are related to memory, the material of it that is eventually repressed, unconscious or that is actually moving from the subconscious to the conscious. In deep meditative contact to these points, it is possible to get in touch with forgotten or repressed memories.

16-18 Etheric points on the back of the head and in the centre of the head

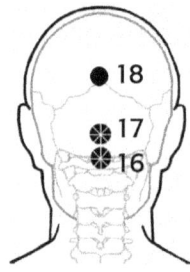

18 Centre of head
17 Blend point
16 Medulla

This illustration of the back of the head shows the point above that is called the blend point and the one under it is the medulla.

16 Medulla

Location: The medulla is located above the neck pit.

Function: The positive function of the medulla is manifested when a person communicates about things that he or she really cares about. So there is often an negative function this point is the place where stress can really be settled. It is also the place where blockages that are related to rejection sit. The medulla point is also called the desire point. Here, "desire" should be understood more in terms of genuine, inner needs. If these real, internal personal needs are suppressed, for example, because of fear of being rejected and condemned, a person can have problems in this area in the form of more or less constant pressure in the back part of the head. This kind of anxiety can be very profound and often unconscious. When genuine need is expressed freely and without fear, outward movement of energy occurs from the medulla area, which signifies freedom of expression. Problems in the medulla area often have a connection to the Hara Chakra.

17 Blend Point

Location: The blend point is located approximately 2 cm above the medulla point.

Function: The blend point is a meeting point of the lower and the higher mental aura, hence its name. Coordination between higher and lower forms of thought forms takes place in the blend point, which is the main coordination point. Awareness points and the silence point also have other functions apart from coordination.

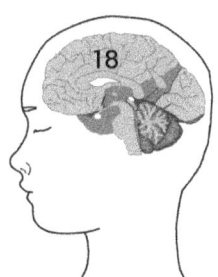

The illustration shows the location of the centre in the head.
The white area is the head's centre filled with liquid where the pituitary gland near the eyes is located.
The pineal gland is located at the rear end of the cavity.

18 Centre in the head

Location: The centre in the head is located between the interbrain deep in the centre of the head and a fluid-filled cavity where the pituitary gland (close to the eyes) and pineal gland (at the back of the cavity) are located.

Function: This point plays a central role in all mental processes. This is the point the mental stream of thoughts arises from. Etheric radiance of the mental train of thought passes through the points on the side of head, far out to the mental control points, outside the edge of the mental aura, when it is optimal.

19-30 Etheric points around torso, arms, front and back

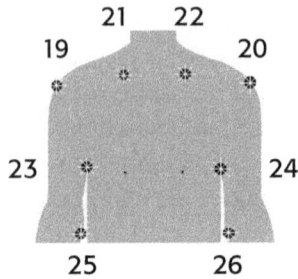

19-20 Shoulder points
21-22 Collarbone points

23-24 Entrance to armpits

25-26 Inner side of elbow

19-20 Shoulder Points

Location: Shoulder points are located at the mid-shoulder rounding at transition between bone and muscle.

Function: The right and left shoulder points are polarity points. The left point is the strongest and is significant for the ability to include a person's innate qualities from the spiritual aura into common life. The right shoulder point relates more to emotions. For both points, it is usual for the mental aura to go through them. A person's contact to the innate balance in the mental aura are particularly expressed in the shoulder points. Shoulder points are also pair points in the great masculine etheric stream covering the entire body.

21-22 Collarbone points

Location: The right and left collarbone points are located approximately in the middle of the collarbone on a straight line parallel to the sides of the neck

Function: The collarbone points are related to events that occur during birth and in childhood. In these points, there can be deposits of a lot of restrained emotions that might cause respiratory problems and difficulties in being able to express ourselves.

23-24 Entrance to armpits

Location: These points are located on the right and left entrance to armpits on the edge of the large pectoral muscles.

Function: These points are related to the heart energy. If there are blockages in the Heart Chakra, in relation to self confidence, the energy stream into these points can be weakened and that can lead to blocked energy flow towards the thymus, having an impact on the immune system and in turn causing decreased energy supply to lymph glands under the armpits.

25-26 Inner sides of elbows

Location: These points are located just below the large elbow bone. Some people find that it is like getting a small electric shock when you press on the elbow(s).

Function: These points are also called temperature points. One can actually press the points in order to reduce body temperature a bit if it is too high. Otherwise, these points are related to both heart energy and the solar plexus area and the ability to manifest ourselves.

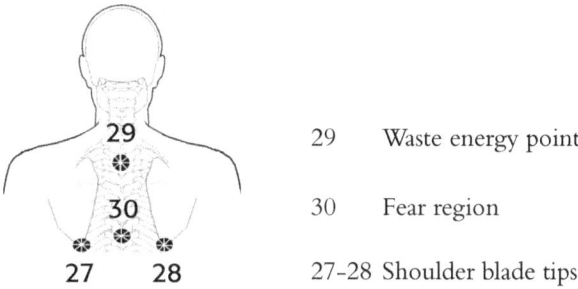

29	Waste energy point
30	Fear region
27-28	Shoulder blade tips

27-28 Shoulder blade tips

Location: These points are located on the left and right shoulder tip. The points are easiest to find after the tips of the shoulder blades have been found. Then you continue about 1 cm up along the shoulder blade edge, towards the spine.

Function: These points are part of the great etheric stream, the so called masculine stream. This masculine etheric stream runs on the outer side of the body and involves both shoulder points and also shoulder blade tips. The shoulder blade tips are also part of the very vital liver stream. When they are in function, the respiratory function is easy and without any obstacles. But in case we have problems with these points, our respiration is often superficial, as if we cannot get enough air into our lungs.

29 Waste energy point

Location: The waste energy point is located on the second thoracic vertebra at the very top of the back. Find the large seventh vertebra that is usually sticking out a bit on the bottom of the neck at the rear of the neck. Search with your fingertips down the spine. Find the first thoracic vertebra and then the second vertebra.

Function: Waste energy is a special term related to this point. Things we cannot express - may they be repressed or suppressed feelings and thoughts – are deposited at the bottom of the body, around the bottom of the coccyx, by the coccyx point. Energy is accumulated there and from time to time it flows up the spine, in the direction of the Throat Chakra and expression. But since it cannot be expressed, it gets deposited around the second thoracic vertebra as a kind of waste energy. This accumulation of energy can be seen in the auric way as a hump on the upper part of the back where physically it can cause problems with tension in the neck and shoulders, in teeth and jaws and that can cause headaches and vision defects. To get in touch with these troubles you can do the following healing exercise with a partner (you cannot do it alone) in order to remove the energy hump on the back and thereby creating balance in this body area and also letting the waste energy loose. This healing exercise with a partner was created by Bob Moore, a specialist in this particular area. See the exercises section in chapter 4.

30 Fear region

Location: Between the shoulder blades centred around the seventh thoracic vertebra.

Function: When there is much fear and great inner tension in a person, in the auric sense an accumulation of energy in the shoulder blade area occurs very soon. It is an auric energy hump that refers to a person's unrecognized emotions. The healing exercise with a partner is not helpful here in the same manner as it is for the waste energy point. It is necessary for the affected person to be psychologically confronted with his or her own so-called shadow aspects. The more emotional shadow aspects are recognized, the smaller the energy hump on the back will be.

31-40 Etheric points of the phrenic area, abdomen and pelvis

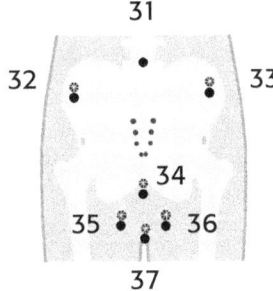

31   Navel
32-33 Hip bone points

34   G-spot
35-36 Inner thighs
37   Perineal point

31 Navel

Location: Slightly above the middle of the belly where the umbilical cord is cut and tied up in newborns.

Function: This area is related to the fetal stage of our existence, birth and the period immediately after birth, and also to mother and father. Many emotional ties are deposited in this area of the body, and experience shows that many people are unable to feel this part of body. It is, for example, easy to bring one's attention to his or her hands. But it is more difficult when it comes to the navel area. If one has trouble with establishing emotional contact to the navel area, it is possible that consciousness is suppressing strong emotional impulses. If there are suppression mechanisms in connection with the navel area, usually consciousness will switch off or forget what it is doing at that particular moment, and then, after a little while, it wakes up. We have to accept this. In connection with this kind of suppression mechanism, we should never push anything through that is, besides, extremely difficult. In case of a meditative exercise, a person has to accept it and start again at the point or body area where consciousness switched off and then attempt to finish the exercise. This applies to all points and body areas where there are possible suppression mechanisms, blockages or imbalances present.

32-33 Hip bone points

Location: Hip bone points are most easily found by putting your fingertips along the hip bone on the front of the body. You should place the fingertips one to two finger widths towards the middle of the belly and 1-2 cm down towards the groin.

Function: These points on the right and left are important polarity points for the whole abdominal area and legs. They are provided with etheric life energy from the Hara Chakra. By using these points correctly, it is possible to achieve greater peace around and in the Hara Chakra and downwards in the legs, which psychologically creates peace of mind and emotions, and even stress and turmoil in the head can be eliminated in this way.

34 G-spot

Location: The G-spot (named after the American sexologist Grafenberg) is located on the inner upper part of the pubic bone where it can be contacted mentally. Physical contact with the G-spot can be achieved inside the vagina and this point naturally exists only in women.

Function: The G-spot is connected to sexuality and the female orgasm. We are speaking of the type of orgasm involving the entire etheric field in contrast to the type of orgasm that only involves the area around the genitals. The G-spot is connected to both spirituality and the woman's contact with earth and their relationship to each other. This point is also responsible for the balance between masculine and feminine energy. In men, the below-mentioned perineal point is used instead.

35-36 Points on the inside of thighs

Location: On the right and left inside of the thighs, in the groin, there are the points located just behind the large tendon, on the inward-leading muscle of the thigh (Adductor magnus).

Function: These points are connected to the energy in the Hara Chakra.

37 Perineal point

Location: This point is located midway between the rectum and the genitals.

Function: This point has a similar function as the G-spot has in women.

38-39 Thrust points

Location: These points are located on the back of the body, on the hip ridge edge, level to the upper edge of the sacrum.

Function: They are called thrust points because when they are active, they create an upward-oriented thrusting motion in the etheric energy.

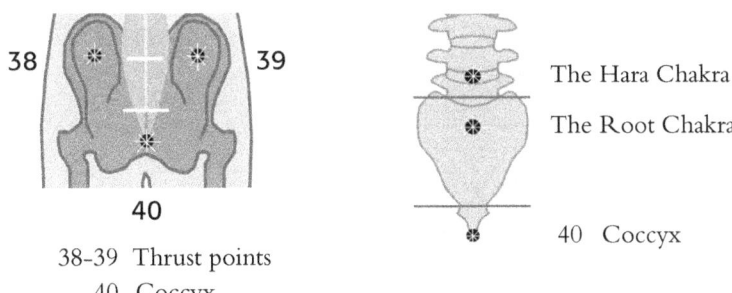

38-39 Thrust points
40 Coccyx

The Hara Chakra
The Root Chakra
40 Coccyx

40 Coccyx

Location: The coccyx point is located at the bottom of the tailbone (coccyx). The tailbone consists of cartilage, an extension of the eight connected vertebrae of the sacrum. The tailbone ends approximately 1-2 cm above the anus on the back of the lower body. The coccyx point is located about 1 cm higher on the inner part of the coccyx that is part of the front of the body.

Function: This point seems to be energetically connected to both the Root and the Throat Chakra. Suppressed or repressed emotions, which a person cannot find words or expression for, tend to be deposited around the coccyx point. It is usually some repressed unconscious material from the time before they had learned a language, meaning from earliest childhood up to 2-3 years of age. These ancient and powerful suppression mechanisms can affect the autonomic nervous system associated with the Root Chakra. Accumulated repressed, unexpressed consciousness can be seen in this area of the body as a light, almost ice blue colour, which shows the connection to the Throat Chakra. The energy moves periodically up along the backbone in the direction of the Throat Chakra when it accumulates too much around the coccyx. This happens in order to find an expression of one character or another. But because the repressed material in consciousness often comes from early childhood, a person has no words to express that repressed material. It may be deposited as an incomprehensible deep grief, anger, powerlessness or a feeling similar to these that might be felt for a split second and then disappears. Energetically, an energy hump centred round the Heart Chakra develops and it is located on the back of the body at the second thoracic vertebra of the spine. This energy hump causes a variety of problems in this body area. Shoulders may become hard and stiff and full of tension and muscle stiffness – you can feel a pressure in the cranium: migraine-like headaches, pain in the teeth, flickering in front of the eyes. The repressed unexpressed energy is trying to be expressed in one way or another. All these symptoms fall under a term that we call "waste energy" - waste energy because the energy in the hump cannot serve for anything else but for the existence of symptoms mentioned above.

41-47 Etheric points on legs and feet

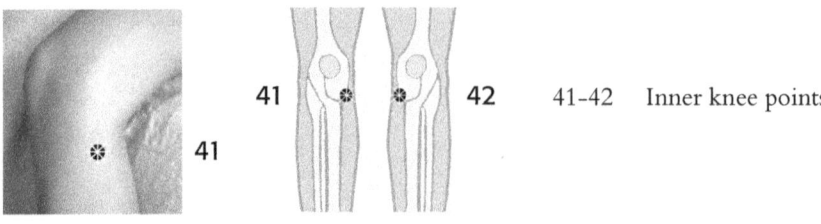

41-42   Inner knee points

41-42 Knee points

Location: The knee points are located on the inner side of each knee just below the bony prominence.

Function: These are the points in the feminine etheric stream that flow on the inside of the legs and thighs and along the centre line of the body and head. The knee points are associated with sexuality and what happened in the crawling stage of a child.

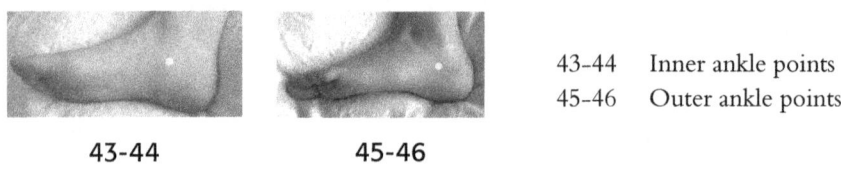

43-44   Inner ankle points
45-46   Outer ankle points

43-44 Ankle points (inner)

Location: The ankle points are located in the middle of a straight line between the inner ankle and the tip of the heel.

Function: Both of the inner ankle points on the right and left foot are etheric points in the feminine etheric stream. They have great importance for connecting to the earth and sexuality and they are associated with the Hara Chakra.

45-46 Ankle points (outer)

Location: The outer ankle points can be localized in the same way as the inner ankle points but just on the outside of the ankle.

Function: The outer ankle points are located in the masculine etheric stream that flows on the outer side of the body. They are significant for connecting to the earth and sexuality and are related to the Hara Chakra.

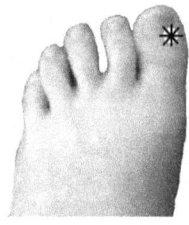

47-48   Point on the big toe

47-48 Point on the nail of the big toe

Location: These points are located on the nail of the right and left big toe in the bottom corner of the nail facing the other foot.

Function: These points are located in the great etheric stream that flows on the inner side of the body, the so called feminine stream. These points are very important for perception and contact with physical reality and are associated with the Root Chakra and the points below the feet.

Chapter 2
The Archetypal Chakra Symbols

The energetic language of consciousness and energetic field

Introduction to the energetic language of consciousness

The Pineal Chakra and its archetypal symbols

The Throat Chakra and its archetypal symbols

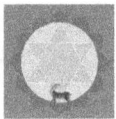

The Heart Chakra and its archetypal symbols

The Solar Plexus Chakra and its archetypal symbols

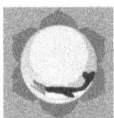

The Hara Chakra and its archetypal symbols

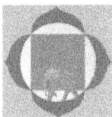

The Root Chakra and its archetypal symbols

Night dreams and personal development

Introduction to the energetic language of consciousness

For trained meditative consciousness or for clairvoyants, different layers of consciousness appear in the form of colours and symbolism, etc. This also applies to archetypal symbols of the seven primary chakras. For less meditatively trained and non-clairvoyants these symbols and colours appear as inner pictures when they are relaxed, when they meditate or when they are dreaming at night.

All inner symbols and pictures are expression of auric energy on a deeper level of consciousness that shows itself in certain types of symbols and colours, and more or less they can be classified in relation to archetypal symbolism of the seven primary chakras. Through a description of different types of symbolism, the reader can identify his or her symbols from the night dreams, the inner pictures and possible meditations in relation to the chakra system. Each of the seven primary chakras has both positive and negative archetypal aspects. The following part of the books deals with a description of archetypal symbols related to the seven chakras.

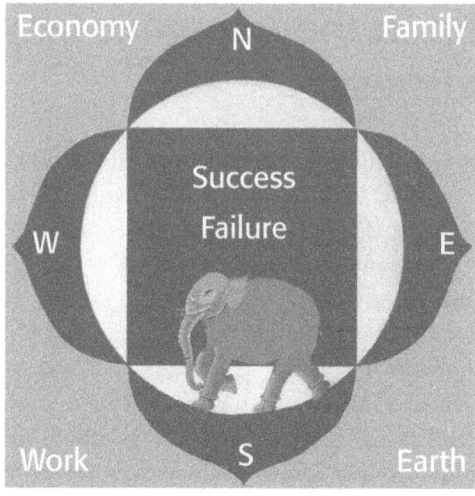

The Root Chakra
and its archetypal symbols

Shapes such as rectangles and squares are associated with the Root Chakra. In India, the Root Chakra is depicted very differently. Mostly, this chakra is depicted as a square, a circle inside it with an elephant. Outside the circle four petals of a lotus flower are depicted. The dormant, mysterious Kundalini in a trance-like sleep is located in this chakra. The figure four is associated with the Root Chakra and with orientation ability. The square and the figure four are used to organise and describe the physical world: the four cardinal directions, the four cardinal points of a clock, the four human temperaments and the four functions of consciousness.

The healthy lifestyle that corresponds with the Root Chakra manifests itself in good housing, finances, work, family relationships, common sense, the stable and functional, soil and solid. The negative aspects are reflected in the sharply defined, seeing the world in black & white, self-limiting, in square opinions, hardness of mind and stiffness.

The earth element
The earth element bounds humans to the ground by gravity. The earth element is the solid foundation we experience from our childhood as the solid and stable in our lives.

Stones and skeleton
Solid material as stone, bone and skeleton symbolically belong to the Root Chakra.

Animal symbols

Elephant, horse, snakes, insects, reptiles, crocodilses, lizards, dinosaurs

These animal symbols are an expression of the instinctive nervous base of the Root Chakra. When these symbols appear in night dreams, meditations and the like, for personal development, it is beneficial to know what these symbols mean and what they want to tell us.

Usually, animal symbols in connection with the Root Chakra are deeply unconscious. This is especially true for animals that are not mammals. If you try to imagine what kind of consciousness form is present in a snake, insect, crocodile, lizard, etc., you can perhaps get a sense of this deep unconscious level. When we encounter these animals in a dream, they are an energetic expression of deep unconscious impulses and emotions that the subconscious is trying to make us aware of. By observing these very deep subconscious signals, consciousness can begin to penetrate deep unconscious emotions of the instinctive animal side of our nature that we usually have no awareness of. This can liberate much of the bound energy useful for other activities.

Elephant and horse

In the Eastern world, the elephant is located in the Root Chakra. The elephant symbolises the great and powerful amount of energy found in this basic field, which is part of man's instinctive autonomous consciousness and autonomic nervous system. It lies as an energy reserve stored in the Root Chakra and in the Eastern world this reserve is also called Kundalini energy, and the survival instinct also has its place there.

The energy is usually used unconsciously and habitually to adapt to life's various vital adaptation processes. As newborns, we have no influence on our lives. The child must adapt itself to parents, environment, society, the times it lives in. This adaptation process demonstrates itself in the autonomic nervous system as habitual behavioural patterns. At a later stage in life, those habitual patterns of behaviour may not be appropriate any more for a person's further development. Life can stagnate in habits and routines.

A human being will progressively become more aware of the large amount of energy bound throughout the whole habitual behaviour. Usually, during routine operations, consciousness enters into the background. If a man attempts for a period of time to be fully conscious of his activities and being as such, there is a change in the habitually bound energy. This energy is transformed into a more alert and creative energy that can inspire new, exciting projects.

When elephants or wild horses appear in dreams, they are an expression of the large powerful energy amounts of our animal consciousness, which is usually bound and invested in adaptation and routine behaviour, which we then have the opportunity to become more aware of.

Snakes

Snakes appearing in dreams symbolise deep unconsciousness. When people begin to get in touch with their deeper levels of unconsciousness, they encounter snakes in their dreams. When the dream-I and the snake come into contact with each other, either the dream-I gets bitten by the snake or the snake turns into an evolutionary higher being (e.g. a mammal or human) and it is the sign of healing in relation to what used to be deeply unconscious.

Snakes mainly symbolise the spinal cord and ganglionic system, which are part of the autonomic nervous system. The autonomic nervous system controls the neural processes that are not subject to will. Dreams about snakes may indicate that a person may have been in contact with the autonomic nervous system during an average day. Snakes appear symbolically in dreams in many different forms. By their colour, you can perhaps get some insight into where they belong in relation to the autonomic nervous system. The colour will show the relation of the autonomic nervous system to one of the seven primary chakras. For example, a green snake may appear in a dream. The green colour is usually associated with growth and the Heart Chakra. If you encounter, for example, a green snake, it could mean that you are beginning to slowly be aware of autonomic nervous reflexes that have formed your behaviour and the contact with yourself and to other people on a deeper emotional level (the Heart Chakra). If you dream about snakes that meander across, for example, reddish brown soil, it could mean that unconscious autonomous impulses are active and can bring you the possibility of becoming aware of these autonomous processes, which in this case are related to the Root Chakra.

The ancient Greek healer and the god of health Asklepios, who is the symbol of medicine, told his patients that they were healed when they had been bitten by a snake in their dream. A personal anxiety often has roots reaching deep into the collective unconscious in the form of four basic types of fear: fear of death, fear of a deadly disease, fear of getting crazy, fear of a deeper sexuality. Deep fears lasting for a long period of time can result in diseases. When you get bitten by a snake in a dream, you have subconsciously overcome your deeper, often strong irrational fear.

Reptiles

There are several types of reptiles related to the Root Chakra and the autonomic nervous system. Reptiles can be apparent in dreams especially during life crises, but they can also occur if awareness has had contact with the autonomic nervous system in some way.

Dreams of crocodiles, lizards and other reptiles occur when the autonomic nervous system is challenged, for example, in the case of turning points in relationships, work, change in career or death in the family. In case of some serious physical illness in which the entire survival potential of autonomic nervous system is activated, in particular large species of dinosaurs can occur in dreams. Contact with dinosaurs in dreams during a life-threatening illness can be crucial in whether a person survives or not.

Insects

Insects in groups may appear in dreams when a specific area of the autonomic nervous system has been particularly affected. Insects can be harmful or beneficial. There are insects that live only on the ground or on plants, other insects fly. For instance, red ants symbolise the social relation of the autonomic nervous system to industriousness and diligence – a person is as industrious as an ant. Large blowflies in a swarm symbolise non-implemented opportunities in the autonomic nervous system that are therefore occupied or attacked by large blowflies and now make use of opportunities that were not energetically utilised. A swarm of bees symbolises movement of life energy. Butterflies refer to transformation in the autonomic nervous system.

Positive condition

When a person has relative order and control over his or her economy, housing, education and employment, when this person mostly experiences joy within family and with colleagues at work, when it is relatively easy for this person to implement his or her projects, when they have a reasonable impact, it all means there is a condition of success in the Root Chakra.

Negative condition

The negative condition in the Root Chakra is having the feeling of failure in relation to work, career, finances, marriage, children, etc.

The sense of smell

The sense of smell is associated with the Root Chakra and the survival instinct. Animals are deeply dependent on their sense of smell. Their survival depends on their ability to smell. The better their sense of smell, the greater their chance for survival. Therefore, smell and the survival instinct of the Root Chakra are two aspects of the same survival mechanism. At the same time, animals are also significantly dependent on smell in relation to their own and other animals marking and demarcation of territory. Without smell, they may simply not orient themselves and would not know where their territory, and that of other animal, is.

People, who have worked with personal and spiritual development for several years, are able to experience wonderful and indescribable scents in relation to their dreams, meditations and in special spaces. Often such types of smell indicate (scents that do not have a physical origin) a socially superior non-physical being whose presence or spiritual energy fills the room with his spiritual fragrance. This type of smell may also indicate that a person has found an attitude to his or her special innate spiritual qualities and their correct usage in physical reality.

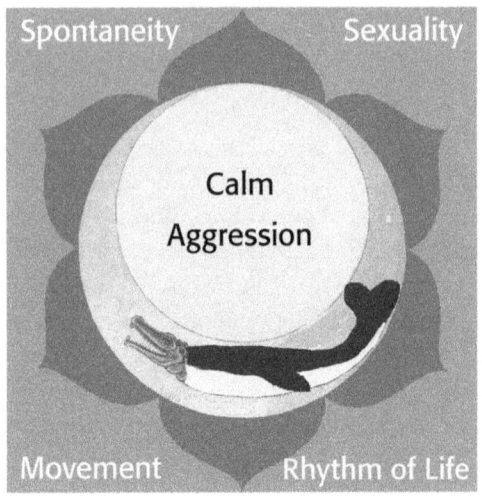

The Hara Chakra
and its archetypal symbols

The geometric symbol of the Hara Chakra is a circle containing a crescent with a mythical animal, which is a mixture between a crocodile and a whale. Swadishthana (the pleasant) as the Hara Chakra is called in Sanskrit, is described as the second centre in the ascending stream of Kundalini. The psychological features of the Hara Chakra are symbolised by the six petals of a lotus flower which surround the circle.

The element of the Hara Chakra is water. Water is liquid and its element fills everything below it. It is a form of energy of being filled that corresponds with the whole. Water also symbolises sexual energy. It is said that humans only use 10 percent of their total consciousness. The remaining 90 percent are in unconsciousness or symbolically filled with water symbolising the unconscious.

The crescent symbolises the phase-like, the rhythmic, and the moody that these comprising energies are creating. The unconscious and the sexual in a person are subjects to different rhythms and phases. The crescent symbol stands for an awareness of these unconscious rhythms and phases. The mixture of whale and crocodile symbolises certain instincts related to the Hara Chakra.

Water element

The Hara Chakra is located in the area of the body where the largest circulation of water in the body, through the kidneys and bladder, takes place. The character of water has many aspects attached to it. C.G. Jung supposed that water was one of the greatest symbols of the human unconscious and that this is, among other things, reflected in night dreams.

Water and human psyche

C.G. Jung ranked dreams about water in different psychological aspects. Water in the form of oceans and seas not surrounded by visible land, are archetypal symbols of what Jung called "the collective unconscious". Lakes, fjords, ponds and wells are archetypal symbols of what Jung called "the personal unconscious". It is worth thinking about this since this symbolises ninety percent of a person's total awareness potential and that it is located in the unconscious.

The inner water in the form of "collective unconscious" and "personal unconscious" represents ninety percent of a person's overall unconsciousness. This means that a human being uses only ten percent of his total consciousness potential. At the same time, our body consists of approximately 60 percent water.

Water has an extraordinary influence on our lives. There is no life without water. Water is a synonym for opportunities of self-realisation. Life arose in water and only much later in the evolutionary process did it conquer land.

Feminine aspect of water

Water is associated with the archetype "The Great Mother" and the life-giving aspect; Mother Nature, mother Earth and the motherly sea. We give water and land a linguistically feminine character. Most deities of sea and earth are female. In her positive feminine aspect, it is the Great Mother with her nurturing, life-giving aspect of all the gentle aspects of life. In its negative feminine aspect, it takes away and sThe Great Mother wants to be treated with great respect and wisdom, otherwise she, like a pendulum, will swing into her opposite negative aspect. Our treatment of Mother Nature over the past century is not something to boast about. It is very likely that we will experience nature from a more damaging perspective.

In the human psychic, inner water and earth are the energy conductive elements, whereas fire and air have an energising feature. It is important for a human being to have balance between energy conductive and energy providing facets of the human inner. This balance concept is called polarity, and in relation to personal development it represents a very important factor.

Animal Symbols

Whale, marine animals, orange-coloured predator, cat, orange-coloured animals

These animal symbols are a depiction of an instinctive, nervous basis of the Hara Chakra. In human dreams, animal symbols may appear that are a mixture of the Root and Hara Chakra, for example, a hippopotamus. The horse is a symbol of the Root Chakra and a hippo will then be a symbol of an animal that is both aquatic and terrestrial, so that is a symbolic animal for both the Root and the Hara Chakra.

All animal symbols are associated with certain parts of the energy field called "the lower astral aura" and are an expression of the human instinctive nervous aspect.

Archetypal animal symbol: whale

In the Western world, the whale is the archetypal animal of the Hara Chakra. In the East, Sanskrit texts place sea creatures in the Hara Chakra. Sea creatures or monsters of the Eastern world are a mixture between a whale and a crocodile. Such a monster is depicted in the ancient Greek myth of Jason, where Jason was swallowed by a sea monster and later he managed to come out of it. Moreover, in the Bible, there is the story of Jonah and the whale.

As mentioned above, animal symbols are an energy depiction of man's instinctive emotional aspects that are associated with the lower astral aura and nervous system. Both a human and an animal instinctively feel what is good or bad for them. If their healthy survival instincts are weakened, wild animals' existence in particular is threatened. In the long term, this also applies to humans.

Positive aspect of whale

The whale's positive aspect is reflected in the human psyche as a very important and healthy instinct that gives us the ability to sense what is healthy and what is unhealthy for us. We could call it the total human health instinct which reflects how we protect ourselves as individuals and as mankind, both mentally and physically. The whale symbolises the ancient healthy survival instincts in every human being who feels what he or she must be wary of. This applies to what we eat and drink, all human relations and working conditions, as well as our ability to sense the natural and that which is created by nature, corresponding with the concept we call natural complementary polarity.

When the environmental organization „Greenpeace" uses a whale's tail as its symbol, it is due to stress the importance that we do not allow our survival instincts and our chances to survive to be weakened by polluting oceans, the atmosphere, through destruction of rainforests, genetic manipulation etc.

When we as mankind act in this way, it reflects a generally poor contact with the healthy survival instinct of the Hara Chakra on a global level.

Negative aspect of whale

The negative aspect of the whale is reflected in emotional submersion. This emotional submersion is called the "archetype of submersion". When we, as individuals and as mankind, go against our inner healthy survival instincts, there is a great risk of emotional submersion. This is what happens to Jonah in the Bible. He goes against God's message to him and becomes a jinx for himself and for others around him. Eventually, he is thrown overboard to alleviate God's anger. In the sea, Jonah is swallowed by a whale. Symbolically, he is psychologically swallowed by his own selfish motives and emotions. In western depth psychology, the image of Jonah in the whale's belly is an archetypal image of submersion.

To overcome this emotional darkness, a person must use his awareness to ignite light. The person needs to find out when he or she goes against his or her inner superordinate character. What is the psychological reason for it? Only through awareness and self-knowledge can a person escape the archetype of submersion. Both Jonah and Jason come out of the whale's belly with deep knowledge that serves as a benefit to society and for their own further development. People who psychologically come out of the whale's belly or escape the archetype of submersion often become heroes of the society, which society needs if it is to develop new sustainable models of identity and ideals in order to survive and develop itself.

Positive condition

Calmness is the positive condition of the Hara Chakra; peace of inner waters and unconscious areas of the psyche. The calm surface of water is a symbol of the quiet observant meditative consciousness that sees the reflection of sky in clear water. When the vegetative nervous system is calm and relaxed, a person is resting within themself. Thus, the person is open to impulses of his deeper superordinate character which it follows consciously or unconsciously. Such a person rests within their body and feels in harmony with their spontaneous impulses that become expressed easily and effortlessly.

Negative condition

If inner waters are in turmoil, it is expressed through inner turmoil, insomnia, deep inner tension, repressed and suppressed anger and aggression, self-blame and self-destructive behaviour with corresponding thoughts and feelings.

If a person is psychically in such a state over a long period of time, they should do something about it. This internal chaos can only calm down through awareness of it and by working with it psychologically. The psychological content can later be the cause of emotional submersion, depression (to be lost in the whale's dark belly), sickness, etc.

It can also suddenly occur after shock, a car accident, a nervous breakdown, drugs and alcohol. To endure this inner turbulent system and to function in it requires large amounts of energy. The only thing that helps is a feeling that you can begin to manage and control these inner forces on your own, but, in most cases, psychological and therapeutic help is required.

When the negative state is dominant in the Hara Chakra, the person does not have much control over his or her emotions and is often forced to suppress them. When they are finally released again, they are often over dimensioned, awkward, distorted and destructive for the person themself. When a person cannot control their inner emotional universe, this person will often try to control other people or even attempt to gain power over others. Power struggles are a reflection of poor balance in the Hara Chakra which is often manifested in relationships between people.

Taste

The sense of taste is associated with the Hara Chakra. Here, we can see a clear link between two chakras. We experience the taste of food and liquids through taste buds of the tongue. The tongue belongs to the Throat Chakra area, so how can taste be associated with the Hara Chakra in the middle of the belly area? On the basis of nerves, we associate taste with either pleasure or discomfort. Feelings of discomfort and pleasure are associated with the Hara Chakra. Good cooking is pleasing and provides us pleasure reaching deep into our soul, but if food tastes horrible, we shudder from discomfort. The Hara Chakra is called "Svadhisthana" in Sanskrit, meaning "the pleasant".

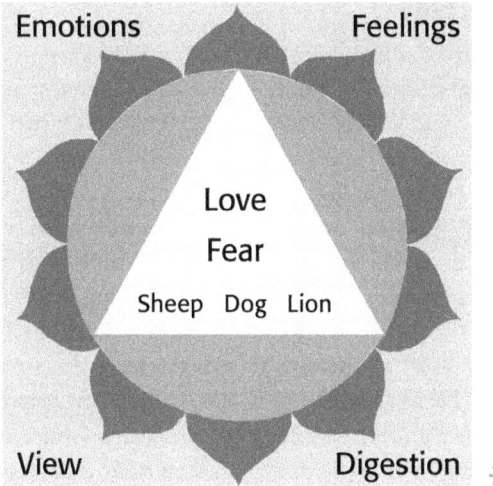

The Solar Plexus Chakra
And its archetypal symbols

In Sanskrit, the Solar Plexus Chakra is called Manipura (gemstone). It is depicted as a lotus flower with ten petals and a triangle in the middle. The symbol describes emotional energies. The triangle is a balance that symbolises the astral emotional energy when it is in balance in relation to the superordinate wholeness symbolised by a circle.

The emotional astral energy is often supreme in human life. In many people, emotions rule over personality without being incorporated into a larger wholeness.

Emotions without deeper meaning and higher perspective, the deeper meaning and function of which is not understood, can have a devastating impact on the balance of the emotional astral system. It is the individual personality's mission in life to become aware of that and then to adapt to its inner higher psychophysical wholeness when a real personal and spiritual growth should be taking place.

The fire element

The element of fire is associated with the Solar Plexus Chakra. The energy rotation and the fire element in the Solar Plexus Chakra are related to the body's inner combustion process and to metabolic processes. On an inner psychological plane the fire element is expressed in certain emotions and states that can be divided into three categories:

1. Destructive aspect of fire
2. Purifying and cleansing aspect of fire
3. Fire as a symbol of the watchful meditative awareness

Destructive aspect of fire

The image of fire that destroys, burns and consumes to keep itself alive is mostly an image of the destructive aspect of emotions. But it can also be an inner dream image of a person's emotional engagement which has been pulled out from the consuming fire.

If emotions are of an explosive and uncontrolled character, without any apparent reason, then this is due to the fact they were suppressed for a long period of time. They were not expressed in situations which usually open up inner emotional impulses. They are an accumulation of suppressed emotions that are deposited in a person's inner; they have the character of a strained spring that is ready to explode on the littlest impulse. The power of fire in such emotional explosions is crucial for how comprising the explosion is. The power of fire in an explosive emotion ignites the whole surroundings. People are quarrelling, shouting, they fight and destroy objects, and they destroy valuable human relationships such as partnerships, marriage, friendships and good relationships with colleagues. A person who cannot control their violent temper and fire power will regularly see the fire destructive aspect reflected in his life. If that person pays attention to such a periodical cycle, he or she will have the opportunity to recognise a certain pattern in such destructive behaviour. The emotional system of a person is mostly periodical. If this is realised and recognised, the person has an opportunity to lower the pressure of inner emotional tension by processing his or her emotions in a more constructive way and thus the affected person is able to achieve bigger and more positive control over them.

Purifying and cleansing aspect of fire

When a human being, perhaps for many years, has been through a process of awareness in relation to his or her destructive emotional behaviour, he or she has been through a purifying and cleansing awareness process. That person managed to achieve control of his or her explosive emotions. He or she has discovered the benefits of not suppressing feelings. The person begins to feel that he or she has control over life. Out of this sense of greater control over life, a feeling of greater self-confidence, self-respect, self-esteem grows. The personal inner strength of faith in a person's self is growing significantly. The inner fire is now expressed as a living dynamic enthusiasm and commitment in all aspects of life.

A person may also realise that the environment will not allow them to express themself freely. For many years, the person may have tried to find some opportunities for personal development. Such a person may at last choose to burn all bridges behind him or her in order to survive and develop as a personality. In such a situation, these burned bridges are a reflection of the purifying and cleansing aspect of fire, but it can also be an indication that the person pulls back from the emotional energy investment and engagement of a life situation. Dreams about fire, for example, a car or working place set on fire, often refer to upcoming changes. Dreams about fire in the form of a burning candle, fire in the fireplace, a campfire, are symbols of transforming and warming aspects of fire which are expressed in a controlled form and means a person has control over their emotions and life.

Watchful, meditative aspect of fire

Fire that is not of a consuming nature is the expression and image of a watchful, meditative consciousness and its higher transformational development aspects. It symbolises the waking, observing consciousness that maintains the meditation process. It quietly permeates emotions by transforming the fire of consciousness and the energy of emotions into a higher development of consciousness. The meditative fire of consciousness can be expressed in dreams and inner symbols, such as a non-consuming fire aura around a meditating person or a non-consuming fire aura burning around a lotus flower.

Archetypal animal symbols:

Lion, dog, sheep and sacrificial animals

Lion - personal strength

For centuries, people have used the lion as a symbol of power and authority in coats of arms, on fronts of houses, castles and palaces. The king of animals is a power and authority symbol that symbolises individual strength, authority, power and control.

When we encounter a lion in a dream or meditation, it is a symbol of this specific type of energy in our inner. The lion is an image of the inner instinctive sense of power and authority, often with a piece of dignity to it. Everyone seeks to gain power and control over their lives through this basic instinct. If a person proves this to themselves and their surroundings, a feeling of dignity arises. They feel their own value - that they are worth something.

By looking at the emanation of the inner lion, we can get a good picture of our relationship with this instinct. When a person has achieved relative control over their life, this instinct, in its later evolution, will search towards the Heart Chakra. A person may begin to understand that everyone should have equal conditions for gaining control and power over his or her own life. The development of a lion-power instinct now turns more in the direction of personal strength and ethics and will also gain more dignity.

With personal strength, the individual faith of a human being is meant and the person's ability to acknowledge this individual faith. The lion instinct is now transformed in the direction of greater humanity and the strength within its own environment. Strength, authority and exercise of power are now serving a common human societal goal. Today, the inner lion in man has become king-like, with great dignity and charisma. The legend of King Richard the Lionheart and his Crusaders is a symbol of the lion and the power instinct that serves some higher thought.

As far as general development of the power instinct is concerned, what matters most is to gain relative control and power over your own life in order for positive sense to be able to evolve in a balanced way. When a person's self-esteem and self-confidence have reached a relative expression in the personal development process, the person feels that he or she now has control and power over their own life. Then the lion archetype is manifested and integrated in connection with the Solar Plexus Chakra. It will now develop in relation to the surrounding society. Development naturally takes place in the direction of greater responsibility to the surrounding society. When the lion and power instinct have come so far in its development, it will be expressed with greater inner dignity and authority and is then integrated in both the Solar Plexus and the Heart Chakra.

Dog – inner alarm

The dog as a symbol is associated with the limit-setting aspect. If a person has ever lived in a house with a dog, they know that the dog barks loudly when the door bell rings or when there is a knock on the door. This image could be transferred into the inner limit-setting instinct. When other people come near us, it is through our inner dog's barking that we become aware that someone is about to cross our borders. This instinct alerts us initially and then we are able to choose whether we will allow that person to come closer. If we do not listen to our inner watchdog, we do not respect it. Without our attention and respect, the inner dog will be cringing as a coward and the same will happen to a person. The person loses self-respect if they do not listen to the limit-setting instinct that the dog symbolises. Respect and attention will be denied. The dog is loyal and man's best friend.

The dog's ancestor is the wolf. If we encounter a wolf in a dream or meditation, it may be the archetype of this limit-setting instinct in its primordial form. This could mean that a person should take a look at his or her limit-setting instincts in relation to family and surroundings, namely in relation to childhood. If such a development process is progressing well, it could provide the basis for a totally new era in human life. The myth of Romulus and Remus who were put out on the Tiber shores just after they were born, and where a she-wolf found them and took care of them, is a myth, where the wolf is heralding a whole new cultural era in world history. The impact of the wolf as a symbol is also seen in the context of various American Indian cultures.

Sheep and sacrificial animals

In India, the Solar Plexus Chakra is symbolised by a mandala drawing of a sheep. When consciousness development is lifted from a flowing state in the Hara Chakra further up the Solar Plexus Chakra, a person becomes aware of the animal "instinctive" functions of emotions that are a hindrance in regards to further development in the direction of the Heart Chakra, and thus, have an impact on a larger humanitarian awareness. Emotions are linked to the animal primordial nature; they are projected on other people in the form of friend or foe, good or bad, black or white, sympathy or antipathy. This life position provides security and clarity, but must be sacrificed in order for a person's further consciousness development to arise. Sacrificial animals symbolise this sacrifice.

The constant judgmental and classifying consciousness that is associated with the emotional life attitude is extensive. To restructure this emotional life attitude (the way of perceiving and experiencing the world), all unacknowledged emotions must be recognised as a person's own. Otherwise, they are automatically projected onto other people. When a person really acknowledges that the reason behind most of all likes and dislikes are their own unacknowledged emotions, he or she begins energetically to understand how much place it fills and occupies in everyday life. The person will slowly begin to become aware of the mechanisms of mind that are responsible for constant judging. He or she now begins to experience and feel their own prior unacknowledged emotions and discover the difference when they are projected or not. The person experiences energy loss when unacknowledged emotions have been projected. The emotional animal heritage of a person's own unacknowledged emotions that are projected must be sacrificed if they want to develop further beyond in order to see the world and people as they really are. It is the only way to remove those rose-tinted glasses.

Positive condition

The positive condition in the Solar Plexus Chakra is the feeling of energy and love. This love's positive mood is a reflection of good self-confidence, self-esteem, self-respect and trust in oneself. When the lower three chakras are functioning acceptably, the energy of the Solar Plexus Chakra will naturally flow up to the heart and the feeling of love.

Negative condition

The negative condition in the Solar Plexus Chakra is fear. Fear is a constricting feeling, while love is an outward-facing expansive feeling. If a person is afraid to express his or her emotions, the cause is fear.

Sight

The sense of sight is associated with the Solar Plexus Chakra. Each human being sees and experiences the world in his or her own way. This is mainly due to the aspects of the Solar Plexus Chakra - sympathy and antipathy. The world becomes divided into what we like and dislike. Every person looks at the world through his or her emotional sunglasses. Some glasses are equipped with blinders and blind spots - a person sees only what they want to see.

All emotional energy affects the eyes and can be deposited as an auric belt around them. If the Solar Plexus Chakra is unbalanced, it will definitely affect sight. If a person becomes ill with a Solar Plexus-related disease, it can also affect the eyes. Diabetic blindness is one such example.

When a person is able to see the world as it is, and no longer sees it as he or she wishes and hopes that it would be, then this person puts down the emotional sunglasses and sees the world in an entirely different light, clearly and sharply. The person's sight and vision is then of an altered quality and this strengthens his or her intellectual, intuitive and mental qualities considerably.

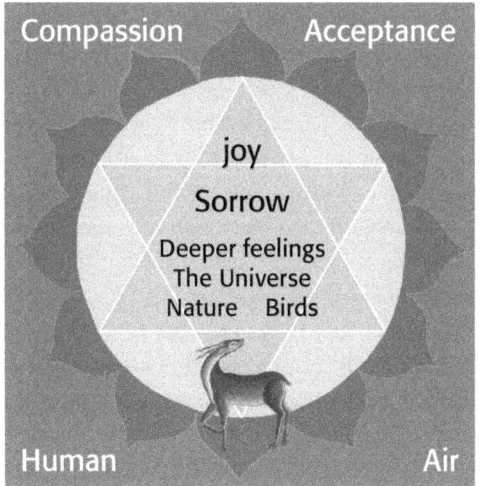

The Heart Chakra
and its archetypal symbols

The geometric symbol of the Heart Chakra symbolises the central balance point of the human being. If individual personality can rest in the Heart Chakra, there will be balance between the personality and its psychophysical whole. In Sanskrit, the Heart Chakra is called Anahata (the unruined) and has twelve lotus petals. The circle symbolises the "Self" as an expression of the comprehensive psychophysical whole. The two triangles symbolise the masculine – the upright triangle pointing upwards – and the female – the downwards-pointing triangle with its downward tip. The geometric symbol of the Heart Chakra reflects balance between the overall psychophysical whole and the masculine and feminine aspect. The Christian cross is also a symbol of balance between the vertical, symbolising the spiritual life and the horizontal, symbolising the earthly life.

Air element - wind

The Heart Chakra is associated with the air element through inhalation and exhalation; the heartbeat's expansion and contraction, diastole and systole of the heart muscle. The moment a baby takes its first breath, a stream of energy from the spiritual, mental, astral and etheric energy field starts to flow into its Heart Chakra.

In this moment the baby encounters and experiences its spiritual dimension associated with its Heart Chakra, for the first time in its life. Later in life, the spiritual dimension is used to lift itself from the physical heaviness and limitation of life.

Through faith, love, art, enlightenment, religion, science, nature and the cosmos, a person strives and elevates him or herself through his search for the spiritual dimension in the inner and outer world.

Dreams about flying are really an expression of aspirations and the ability to lift yourself towards the spirit. Man conquered the physical air element long ago, but as far as the inner air element is concerned, we still have a long journey ahead of us. Most of mankind identifies itself more with their body than with their consciousness and spirit.

People who are centred in the Heart Chakra and thus in the air element identify themselves naturally with spiritual principles and qualities. This is expressed through practice of these spiritual principles that are validated in activities and deeds of everyday life. In the Heart Chakra man is uniting the physical with spiritual, yin with yang, feminine with masculine. It is the place where opposites meet and unite. The Heart Chakra is man's natural balance point.

Animal symbols

Antlers and deer, unicorns, birds, etc

Antlers and deer

In the Eastern world, a gazelle is depicted, symbolising animals with antlers connected with the Heart Chakra. These fast and light-legged horned animals and deer symbolise fast elusiveness of thoughts in emotions that are tied to the instinctive thought processes in the lower mental aura. Autonomous uncontrollable rushing of thoughts lies in dependency and identification with the instinctive, lying as an unconscious background in the lower mental aura.

The task of a person is to consciously disassociate himself or herself from this identification with the instinctive. Antlers of deer and the unicorn's horn are used to symbolise the antennae and opportunities of a human being for development in a spiritual direction. To approach the spiritual, a person must learn to control the speed of thought flow. This can be done through the training of the mental system through, for example, meditation, prayer and other exercises.

C.G. Jung often stated that an archetype has two aspects: instinct and spirit. In the instinct of our animal nature lies the antenna-like option, the opportunity for transparency, so that the divine, the spirit can be received clearly. The human ego with its emotional, instinctive mental thought processes can be an antenna for the higher.

Birds

Most birds dominate the air space and therefore are associated with the Heart Chakra. They symbolise again thoughts or the mentally instinctive. If a person encounters a bird in inner pictures, dreams and meditation, thye should look at its mode of life and especially its colour, to find out its symbolic meaning. The birds' colour often suggests a connection with a respective chakra. Black birds, such as a raven, rook or crow might symbolise heart properties that are not particularly conscious (black) and exist due to a too strong identification with the emotional. A white bird, for example, a seagull, flying rapidly away perhaps symbolises a pure thought in volatility of the mental system, whereas a white seagull floating balanced in the air, could symbolise a balance of thoughts.

It is important to look at a bird's colour. The colour will always indicate a connection to a different chakra and body area. For example, a turquoise bird will be associated with the area of the body between the Heart and Throat Chakra. When green (the Heart Chakra) and blue (the Throat Chakra) are mixed, turquoise is the result. In the area of the body between the two chakras, the secondary chakra of thymus is located and has a significant influence on the immune system. If a person is not able to defend and express his self-consciousness, it will affect the immune system. This leads to a possible compensatory appearance of a turquoise bird in dreams in order to eliminate this imbalance. A turquoise bird appearing in dreams could also possibly mean an opportunity for a greater feeling of freedom (free as a bird), emotions of expansion and greater authenticity towards oneself and the outer world, since turquoise is the symbol of honesty.

Positive condition

The positive condition of the Heart Chakra is a deep inner feeling of joy arising from love and a feeling of joy for life as such, of nature with all its creatures, the world and the cosmos. It is the joy of giving and sharing love, a feeling of unity with other people and nature.

Negative condition

All people experience grief in some period of their life. Grief is often painful and therefore, a person often closes down from it. It will be suppressed and thus become a part of many people's daily mood. Many people are not really happy because they have shut down from their grief. If joy is going to be a part of life, grief must also have its space and expression. By expressing sorrow joy can be awoken.

Sense of touch

The human sense of touch and sensitivity are attached to the Heart Chakra. All people are born sensitive and with a sense for sensitivity. Children are more sensitive than adults.
Most adults experience smells, tastes, colours and atmospheres from times of their childhood much stronger when they go back to these in their memory. Much of information that a child receives from its surroundings, get through to him or her

through its sensitivity. It senses the atmosphere of its surroundings and environment and that's primarily what a child is influenced by. If there is accordance between what the child senses and the information it receives from parents and surroundings, it has good chances to develop a good sensibility and sensitivity.

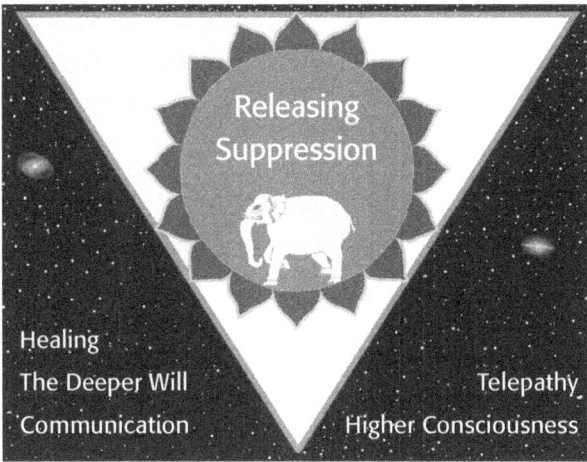

The Throat Chakra
and its archetypal symbols

In Sanskrit, the Throat Chakra is called Vishuddha (the Pure). There are sixteen lotus petals associated with the Throat Chakra. The geometric illustration of the Throat Chakra shows a downward pointing triangle with a base line above and a circle in the center of the triangle. The triangle represents the trinity aspect from a cosmic perspective, the psycho-physical unity of man, and all of that framed in a circle. It represents the higher consciousness perspective of the Throat Chakra seen from the cosmic context. The white elephant represents a notion of equality between the earthly material reality and the spiritual reality.

Element: Sound

The sound element and the human voice are linked to the Throat Chakra. The sound element is related to the etheric element, which according to the ancient Indian wise, the Rishi, created the underlying elements of air, fire, water and earth. On a divine level, the creative power of the sound element appears as the sound of cosmos, celestial music, cosmic choir of the universe. On a more earthly plane, it is expressed as divine music, church choir, sounds of bells.

Experience of the sound element on the energetic level corresponds to a higher conscious level or the divine, where things correspond from their cosmic and universal perspective; the feeling that all is carried by a basal universal cosmic vibration, which permeates time and space, everything and everyone is of cosmic character.

The creative power of the sound element is also expressed in the Bible in the Gospel of John in the following words: "In the beginning was the Word, and the Word was with God, and the Word was God".

On the scientific level, one of the most respected scholars of the 20th century, George Ivanovitch Gurdjieff presented his views related to all forms of vibration which he considered to be a trinity of wave, pulse and form. He saw these three basic principles as a fundamental force and the law behind all creation phenomena. He said: "There is a law - the law of trinity. It is the law of three fundamental principles or three main causes - wave, pulse and form, the fact that all phenomena, no matter on what scale, in which world or reality they exist, from a molecule up to cosmic phenomena, are the result of a combination of these three basic principles."

The Swiss scientist, inventor and musician Hans Jenny (died in 1972) was the founder of Cymatics - the study of visible sound and vibration and of the effect of sound waves on physical substances. He discovered that through their vibration, sound waves produced certain patterns and figures in physical substances. If he changed the sound frequency, changes in figures and patterns occurred.

On a cosmic level, the divine vibration is behind or beyond all forms of vibration. The word of God exists beyond words and ideas in the depth of the heart of every human being, and there is a direct link with the divine love and divine will. On this basis, beyond all words, a prayer from the heart from all religions was created. We are all part of creation, so we all have a spark of divinity within us that allows us to harmonise with that will.

If we, in a religious sense, believe that we are here on the earth due to the omnipresent God's will, it is also the largest purpose of life to live in harmony with God's word and will.

Through prayer, meditation and similar practices, man has tried for thousands of years to find harmony with the ineffable and transcendental points inside the heart. A person works, perhaps throughout their whole life, in a goal-oriented manner to achieve the sound of silence, the place where all sounds have their origin and destination. Stillness is a transcendental meditative state where the mind rests in a neutral state of non-dual unity, which is the initial and final point of all forms of movement and vibration.

Animal symbols

White horse and white elephant

The seed of higher consciousness arises from the Throat Chakra. Higher spiritual awareness is now no longer subordinate nor weaker compared to the general materially dependent self-consciousness. The Throat Chakra is the transition to a different order, a higher common denominator for matter and mind. The white elephant and the white horse symbolise the equal relationship between mind and matter.

The immaterial, spiritual experience of reality is as real here as the material, physical reality. Therefore, the elephant appears in a higher octave. Now the grey elephant of the Root Chakra and of the rest of animal instinctive area has been made transparent, lit through by light and consciousness, and, therefore, it is represented by the white elephant / white horse.

There is no other animal symbolism and there are no forms of duality above the Throat Chakra. In the higher form of consciousness of the two upper chakras (the Pineal Chakra and the Crown Chakra) all duality is transcended into unity.

Positive state of the Throat Chakra: Redemption

When the energy flows and is balanced in the Throat Chakra, it will have a redemptive effect on the environment around it. In order to maintain balance in the Throat Chakra, three things are required:

1. To work with the body daily and aim at eliminating possible accumulated emotions.
2. To express emotions and feelings and release them.
3. To scan the mental system daily, e.g. through meditation.

It takes time to come so far. Once this is achieved, this state can be maintained without much trouble. It only requires a little self-discipline and focus.

Negative state of the Throat Chakra: repression and oppression

Most people are unresolved in some measure. You can be unresolved in two ways: either by an unconscious emotional mental suppressive mechanism or you carry unresolved pain in your own inner and have to face it. A person who represses and oppresses, carries a burden on their shoulders and has a bowed head, while those who take responsibility upon themselves, carry that load with raised heads. An unresolved person will always seek release, consciously or unconsciously.

Sense: hearing

Ears and the hearing sense are associated with two secondary chakras called the "right and left ear".

Hearing is the first developed sense that starts to be active in the fifth month of the fetal stage. The fetus hears the voice of its mother, pulse of the heart, roar of the blood in her veins and noises produced by the stomach and the digestive system of its mother. These sounds reach the brain of the fetus through sound vibrations through the amniotic fluid of the fetus and enter its eardrum, where different sound vibrations are processed by its brain.

Particularly, the sound of the mother's voice has a stimulating effect on the brain of the fetus and it is decisive for how the child will communicate later in its life. This has been discovered by the French ear and throat specialist, surgeon and inventor Alfred A. Tomatis. He has made revolutionary discoveries and during the past 50 years he has redefined the importance of hearing and ears. Our ability to communicate is already formed during our intrauterine development. If we experience sounds in terms of certain traumatic events, we block off the sound frequencies that we associate with such traumatic experiences. Tomatis has developed a music therapy related to this problem and has achieved excellent results with it.

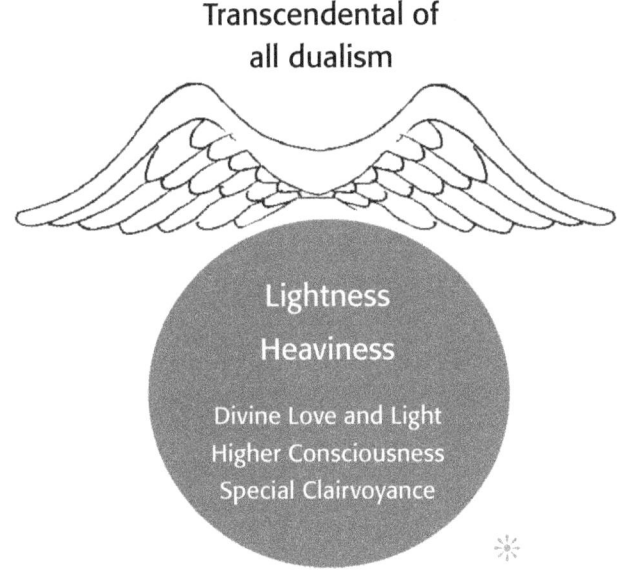

The Pineal Chakra
and its archetypal symbols

Ajna (the dominant) is the name of the Pineal Chakra in Sanskrit. Wings on the illustration symbolise transcendence, which is finally transformed in the direction of cosmic consciousness. Wings symbolise the ultimate transcendence of various dual poles. Language is no longer enough; its meaning was created on multiple dualities.

Element: Light

Lighting element is associated with the Pineal Chakra. The pineal gland inside the head is the only physical organ that contains light-sensitive cells. Human consciousness is symbolized by light. Every person is connected with a higher form of consciousness. This higher form of consciousness is an inner higher spiritual / cosmic community that is symbolised by the light of the world, Jesus Christ, Buddha, Krishna, Allah and other religious founders.

Usually, a person dreams one or two dreams from this higher consciousness area every year. Such a Pineal Chakra-related dream will appear more real and alert than the normal, daily conscious, awake state. Such dreams contain a lot of light, full of concentrated information that is of a visionary and deeply intuitive nature, through which higher consciousness communicates, forming the ordinary human consciousness, perhaps for several years. The stronger and clearer the light is, the higher the form of consciousness.

The Pineal Chakra sound
The sound associated with the Pineal Chakra is the ancient Indian, 12,000 year-old sound Om. The sound is pronounced OOUUMM. When the sound is articulated correctly, it should activate light and consciousness. Therefore, this sound should be used with caution if a person does not have a lot of years of knowledge of their own personal development. This sound is used both in India and in Tibet and is considered to have great spiritual influence.

Animal symbols
There are no animal symbols associated with the Pineal Chakra.

Positive state: lightness
The Pineal Chakra influences the whole mental field. Light and clarity in mental thought processes create an atmosphere of lightness around people who have this mental contact. In a person who does not exclude light and consciousness from his or her inner space, the atmosphere of light will prevail, giving an aura of lightness. When we speak of consciousness on that level, consciousness is in direct relation to love. Therefore, it is never a cold form of consciousness. A unity of feelings of cosmic love is the motivation and driving force in all consciousness-illuminating cognition.

Negative Condition: Mental heaviness
If the mind influenced by internal conflicts between consciousness and withheld thoughts, emotions and feelings, there is a reduction of natural innate ease, leading to a feeling of excessive demands, destructive heaviness and depression-like states.

There is no archetypal symbolism associated with the Crown Chakra, except of the divine guidance of the principle of unity by the all-pervasive and omnipresent power of cosmic love.

Dreams – Self-development - Energy Field

Function of dreams

We all have a natural built-in regulator that balances our inner psychic life. Night dreams, daydreams and fantasies belong to this inner psychic balancing regulator. If a person is not allowed to dream, the psychological borders of such a person will eventually break.

Sigmund Freud and C.G. Jung called night dreams the royal road to a person's subconscious. They discovered that dreams, mostly, are compensatory for reality. If a person is too good and kind-hearted in daily life, then in such a person's night dreams, his or her so-called dark side appears in the form of unkind and nasty people trying to come in contact with the dreamer. Conversely, if a person is too unapproachable, unfriendly and offensive, gentler sides of his or her character appear in their dreams. Dreams are constantly trying to balance our psyche through also, for example, daydreams, fantasies and play.

This inner psychological health regulator is of the highest value for people. When people suddenly become sick, it is often because this inner health regulator is suffering some disorder. It may have been ignored and neglected for years before a physical disease broke out. By knowing the ancient universal language of dreams, a person is far better equipped to face the challenges that modern life demands.

Dreams and the energy field

Dreams have a direct connection to the astral energy field and therefore belong there. The condition that a person usually finds himself or herself in during dreaming is an astral consciousness form. Characteristic for the astral state of consciousness is the dreamer's borders being far more blurred, more open and diffuse than in a normal awake consciousness state. In an awake consciousness state these borders are sharp, they have a borderline and are much more closed. The awake consciousness state during the day differs from the astral consciousness form in that there is much greater clarity and light present. In the astral dream state, there is less clarity and light present in consciousness. When consciousness is dreaming in the open astral dream state, it allows the unacknowledged and demerged personality parts to reach consciousness. Dreams can be divided according to different layers of consciousness of the energy field, but will always have the astral dream state as a starting point. Dreams can be divided according to their relevance to etheric, lower and higher astral dimensions, to mental or spiritual dimensions.

By learning the symbolic language of different auric layers of consciousness, it is much easier to find orientation in these and obtain an insight into how a person uses their life and time. Below, many archetypal symbols that belong to different layers in the energy field are going to be presented. These symbols may provide readers with a glimpse into how night dreams correspond with the human energy field, but they are by no means a complete picture, they are just an appetiser for readers to search for further information in case they are interested.

Dream mechanism and the lower three chakras

Eighty-five percent of all night dreams come from the lower three chakras: the Root, the Hara and the Solar Plexus Chakras. These dreams aim to enable the dreamer to be aware of certain emotional, sexual attitudes and emotions that are unconscious for the dreamer.

It is also important to understand that all the aspects and objects that we encounter in dreams, are partial aspects of ourselves. It may be unrecognised emotional, sexual aspects and motifs in our personality that we encounter in dreams, personality aspects which we cannot identify ourselves with and therefore must encounter them in a compensatory way through dream mechanism. In the case of positive and negative unacknowledged personality parts, people tend to project them onto others and thereby create problems or challenges. By turning these unacknowledged personality parts into being aware and integrated, the dream mechanism will be liberated from performing this activity and the liberated energy will naturally manifest itself in a greater quality of life on all levels.

Working with dreams in relation to personal development

Working with dreams happens in three major psychical areas. The first and most common area is the shadow - the unacknowledged emotions that trigger affects. The other major psychical area is anima and animus - woman in man and man in woman. The third is inner wisdom or inner guidance.

C.G. Jung stated that integration of the shadow in connection with personal development could be seen as a fellow part, while integration of anima / animus could be regarded as a master piece. It says something about how much experience and maturity is needed to integrate anima / animus. If we understand that we can develop ourselves by means of dreams and we integrate different personality parts, from time to time we can experience a so-called wisdom dream which is a direct guidance from the inner part of us in relation to personal development.

The shadow

In a person's dreams, the shadow is the same sex as the dreamer. It is usually a person who can bring the dreamer into a strong passion-filled emotional state – for example, the dreamer can get into a panic, to do something uncontrollable, to do something totally irrational. This part of the personality is called the shadow, because it lies in darkness and unconsciousness of personality, thereby it has power to bring the dreamer into an emotional excitement. This unconscious emotional response can easily be transferred to a concrete reality. There will be areas of emotional character the dreamer avoids on a daily basis, areas he or she ignores or turns his or her back on. It can be an area the dreamer looks upon as reality through a prism of fear and emotions. Due to unconscious emotions and fear the person is not able to see clearly. This is the aspect the shadow wants to call the dreamer's attention to in night dreams.

For a person who works with his or her dark sides, they have a duty to learn to recognise these uncontrollable emotional sides as his or her own. Working with the shadow consists of more development segments, which can be divided into three areas related to dreams:

1. Dreams of an unknown stranger of the same sex who brings the dreamer to excitement without any physical contact between them. (To have physical contact with the shadow in dreams means greater contact and more awareness in reality)
2. A familiar person of the same sex where there is physical contact between the shadow and the dreamer. This meeting usually ends in a conflict where the dreamer and shadow fight - often a life and death fight.
3. The dreamer and the shadow become friends, or the shadow dissolves in the midst of a battle and confrontation with the dreamer, which indicates integration and cooperation.

For further progress to be possible, the first part of the shadow work is to recognise the excitement triggering the fear impulse both in the dreams and in the physical reality. The next development will be confrontation with the shadow.

Confrontation

In working with the shadow, the focus is on confrontation rather than escape and turning away. The attitude a person has in real life will be mirrored in the dream life. Shadow dreams will always reflect the degree of contact between the dreamer and the shadow. The greater contact between the dreamer and the shadow, the stronger the confrontation will be with the shadow in concrete reality. The less contact between the dreamer and the shadow, the less the confrontation will appear in reality. The personal and mind-stimulating work of the confrontation of the shadow in daily life will release a lot of energy in dream mechanism. The released energy will be used to achieve integration between the person and the shadow.

Integration

When the dreamer is aware of his or her own shadow-like emotionality in everyday life and that he or she can now begin to control the so-far unconscious emotions before they are turned into conscious, this will be reflected in dreams, where the shadow shrinks or becomes the dreamer's good and helpful friend. When that happens, more psychical energy will be released so that the dream mechanism will face deeper layers of personality. Dreams about the opposite sex can be divided into several stages of development in sexual dreams or in anima / animus dreams. The man's inner woman is his anima, and the woman's inner man is her animus.

Anima / Animus – the opposite sex
Dreams about the opposite sex can be divided into several stages of development in sexual dreams or in anima / animus dreams. The man's inner woman is his anima, and the woman's inner man is her animus.

Sexual dreams and their function
The primary function of sexual dreams is to bring the unconscious and the not fully accepted sexual emotions, sexual tendencies to consciousness. Sexual energy is an aspect of a person's total energy that includes both the personal unconscious and the collective unconscious. Therefore, sexuality is very comprising. It is directly related to the physical body and to all layers of consciousness of the energy field. It is, as long as humans have been present in this world, in motion and variation. If the sexual energy in a person is locked up or obstructed in its natural motion, it can be in the form of taboos, morals and ideals, and if simultaneously there are sexual emotions existing deeper in personality, it will be reflected in sexual dreams or dreams with sexual symbols. If sexual energy will be repressed unconsciously, it will be manifested in other ways and forms. Then man's struggle with sexuality will result in increase of sexuality, finally, everything will be sexualised.

For real personal and spiritual growth to take place, sexual energy must firstly be accepted as completely as possible without any prejudice. Next, the body must be released from stored, accumulated, blocked sexual energy in the muscles as much as is possible.

Dreams about sexuality serve to bring repressed, tabooed or simply overlooked sexuality into consciousness. Dreams can thus help to move sexuality into consciousness and also dream energy can be involved in deeper parts of personality.

All dreams about the opposite sex belong to the anima / animus aspects. However, it is worth only dealing with certain dreams within the anima / animus aspect. When, for example, a man meets a woman, in a dream, whose charisma and appearance has nothing to do with the external reality, his contact to his inner femininity is of a rather perfect character. Jung named a man's inner femininity anima and he named a woman's inner man animus.

Anima dreams are very intense. If a man dreams about the anima, he will always be deeply affected, and the meeting itself in the dream is full of deep fascination. This kind of dream makes a very deep impression on the dreamer as the dreamer is meeting his other half in such a dream.

Similarly, the same intensity will be present when a woman meets the animus in her dream. The inner man will be the prototype that is behind outer infatuations. So the woman is given a detailed picture of the source of infatuation inside herself.

If sexual intercourse takes place in this type of dream, it will trigger a nine-month dream sequence that will result in a dream about birth or rebirth - the fruit of the meeting between the male and female energies.

Polarity is the keyword in connection with anima and animus. There is human induced polarity and natural complementary polarity. Anima and animus are symbols of a person's naturally cooperating complementary polarity that will always be connected with healthy growth. The better a man is able to express and accept his male and female pole, the more he grows as a person. The same applies to the woman. All growth and life has arisen from a naturally cooperating complementary polarity. For spiritual growth, contact to anima and animus is required. Otherwise, no deeper spiritual development can occur.

Wisdom - the inner guide

One of the archetypes in connection with anima / animus is the inner royal wedding, the inner divine wedding. Man and woman can often be guided by their inner anima / animus in this process. It is also not unusual that on this level a person encounters a wisdom figure and receives direct guidance in how to deal with specific questions related to their personal and spiritual growth. The primary role of the wisdom figure is to advise the dreamer in his or her personal and spiritual development.

Wisdom dreams occur aurically when a person's spiritual and astral aura begin to approach each other more consciously. This means that a person starts coming into contact with higher forms of emotions and atmospheres of religious character. When this atmosphere of celebration takes place in the mental astral field, it will usually provoke dreams of wisdom and inner guidance. When this happens, the dreamer can experience it as a figure who is present in the astral field. This process is therefore named figure building in the astral field. If a person enters an atmosphere of celebration he or she invites the inner wisdom. Naturally, a wisdom figure will appear in a dream only if the person's shadow and anima /animus are more or less processed.

The advantage of the inner wisdom dreams is obvious. A human being now obtains, through inner wisdom dreams, direct information in the form of one or more inner guides. At the beginning of the wisdom process, these guides can appear as an external teacher, guru or similar in wisdom dreams. Later, a person's personal inner guide will be replaced by an external guide. Or they will experience the inner guide's speech directly and telepathically.

In this context, the following is important to know: if an external teacher or guru is in direct contact with their own wisdom layer or spiritual field, this will resonate in the astral dream dimension, so the "student" will receive information from this teacher or guru in a dream. Should the student of the teacher or guru not receive any information through the dream channel, then the teacher or guru almost certainly is not in touch with his own wisdom layer or spiritual field. A person should of course take into consideration possible reticence towards wisdom, especially if they have suffered a strong emotional trauma, and the like, which the shadow mechanism closes the door on and does not allow wisdom to approach.

The inner guide is also associated with what we call our guardian angel, because of the solemn feeling and feeling of light that follow these dreams. When a person has first made contact with wisdom, it may also be reflected in direct information during meditation.

Direct guidance in meditation is not rare. This kind of guidance will usually have a spiritual goal. It can be of an ethical character or of a higher consciousness.

To approach higher states of consciousness in a balanced state, a person should either have an external teacher who can already operate in higher conscious states, or an inner teacher who is already familiar with a higher conscious state.

Auragrams and dreams

Jes Bertelsen has developed a technique that shows the energy field in its symbolic form. This technique is described in details in his book "Dreams, Chakra Symbols and Meditation." This technique is called 'auragram'. If you are interested in seeing your own energy field in symbolic form, you can draw it on an auragram. An auragram is a sketch on a piece of paper of which the physical body is outlined. Over a period of six months, you draw, precisely, various powerful symbols and colours that have had a big impression on you in your dreams. These symbols and colours are drawn in and around the outlined physical body according to where the various dream symbols belong in relation to the chakra system. After half a year you will get an auragram which is a symbolic reflection of what is going on in your energy field.

If you have trouble placing the symbols and colours in and around the body, then you might first try to feel which part of the body they could belong to. You could possibly also more intensively consider the archetypal symbols and chakras, and also the geometric symbols and chakras, to find out where these symbols and colours belong in relation to the physical body and the seven primary chakras.

Chapter 3
The Astral Energy Field

*The illustration shows the astral energy field (emotional body)
that surrounds the physical body like an egg,
stretching in diameter, on average, about 30 cm from the physical body.
The astral emotional aura is a moving, multi-coloured energy field
that is very difficult to display on a two-dimensional piece of paper.
The astral energy field can expand and contract
depending on the emotional state a person is in.
The variety of colours of the astral energy
represents a significant part of this chapter
because they give a very accurate insight into what is going on
in a person's deeper feelings.*

The astral energy field

The astral energy field is called the emotional energy field or the feeling body. This is the part of our consciousness where all emotions, feelings and moods are expressed. Our emotions and moods create a layer of atmosphere around us. These moods literally dye what we radiate. We can radiate joy, love, relaxation, tension, excitement, disappointment, uncertainty, concern, honesty, anger, etc. All these moods can be observed and seen as colours in the astral energy field and are called astral colours.

The speed of emotional vibration is higher and finer than the etheric vibrations and can therefore influence the etheric energy field in the positive or negative direction, depending on what type of mood is dominant in a person. Conversely, it is through the astral energy field that people make an emotional contact with a thought, concept, idea, vision or intuition. All human lower and higher consciousness functions have an emotional resonance in the astral energy field.

Development of the astral energy field

Pregnancy

From the 5th or 6th months of pregnancy emotional impulses may be detected in the fetus. It has dream activity and periods when it is physically active. It kicks, as they say, but what is actually happening during such activities, we know very little about. But it is certain that the fetus responds to external sounds.

I'll never forget when I went to an Omnimax film show in a planetarium with my pregnant friend, who was in the seventh month of her pregnancy. The fetus reacted very strongly to the very deep frequencies which were coming out from the big speakers of the planetarium's giant sound system.

Each time the deep sounds were audible, the fetus reacted by kicking very violently. Finally we decided to leave because it was obvious that the little unborn child did not like these deep frequencies.

The mother's state of mind and her emotional contact with the child during pregnancy and after birth is crucial to how the child develops emotionally and mentally in later life.

Birth

It is remarkable to observe the astral energy field of a newborn child. Although the newborn has just been through a very dramatic experience, namely the actual birth, its astral aura is not much affected. Most newborns have a whitish colour in their astral energy field reflecting a unique emotional purity.

From the first breath, a change in colour is going on in the astral energy field and the etheric energy field. This happens for the first time through the respiratory function of the baby's lungs. During pregnancy, the child's etheric aura was provided by the life energy from the mother through the umbilical cord. When the baby's lung function starts to be active, the child's own self-supply of life energy through breathing is activated at the same time. From the first breath, an inflow of two to three shades from the spiritual aura can be observed, flowing through the mental and astral aura and from there into the child's Heart Chakra. This inflow of spiritual energy in the form of high-frequency vibrations of consciousness dyes the baby's higher astral aura with the colour qualities it has brought with itself from its previous lives.

These colours give the child a fixed point and a higher sense of being, so it is possible for the baby to feel "at home" in the middle of all the new things happening with and around it. The baby's physical contact with its mother is very important in this context. It is important for the baby to as soon as possible after birth be placed on the mother's belly before the umbilical cord is cut.

The mother is the child's source of confidence and a fixed point on the outer physical plane and has been this throughout the whole pregnancy. The child's new inner contact to its innate spiritual qualities or the reminiscence of them is its spiritual anchor. The necessary synthesis, trust and integration between the physical and the spiritual happens in this initial time through contact with the mother. Through fundamental and essential needs and situations like breastfeeding, bathing, nursing and care, the baby experiences acceptance of its inner and it leads to a natural synthesis between the spiritual and physical.

This synthesis between the baby's spiritual character and maternal care is necessary for development of trust in own self-confidence of the child. It is through self-confidence that the child is later, in adult age, able to express its spiritual qualities. The child's natural contact with its mother at the physical level, its inner spiritual contact with its innate qualities form the basis for its future natural contact to its deeper identity that is both of spiritual and physical character.

After birth

Personally, I think that it is extremely important to research and cast light on the state of consciousness which the newborn child is in after birth and its first year of life. In our modern world, there should be an institution that would exclusively investigate the phenomena of small children's state of consciousness, since knowledge in this area could contribute to a much greater insight into what and who we humans really are.

By "observing" a child, I have discovered that it is in a kind of condition of unity where consciously it is not able to distinguish itself from its surroundings. It feels as one with its mother, father and its surroundings. A person might ask why children are born with this very high form of consciousness. What is the reason for it? The child is unaware of this high state of consciousness. It has no awareness about the state of consciousness it is in. It is just fully in its being. For me, the child has a kind of higher consciousness, without any form of "self-consciousness", which, of course, is the evolutionary and elemental necessity if you are to succeed in the physical world. The only way to find out what the child is experiencing is by entering the same level of consciousness as the child is on. This level is, as mentioned before, a state of unity, a state where subject and object are partly fused together, as is seen to happen in higher conscious states.

Most people have had a look into a small child's eyes. A small child approaches and faces each person without any prejudice. There is something in its eye that looks at the person in totality and if the person is just a little bit sensitive, they cannot help but be deeply affected by such an encounter. The child's state of unity resonates in the adult consciousness, consciously or unconsciously, and this encounter of two forms of consciousness evokes deep feelings in an adult and could best be described as love.

If the adult feels fear in the case of such an encounter, it is because the child realises and faces split parts in the adult's consciousness, and these parts are either repressed or lay in the unconscious, and the adult consciousness begins to suspect them. Therefore, fear is the resulting feeling. The adult fear can be transmitted onto the child who begins to cry. The small child expresses the adult's unexpressed pain due to split parts of his or her consciousness. The child's pure mind and its undivided consciousness can be a catalyst agent that shows the adult his or her split mind.

Universal language of love

The state of unity uses a common, universal and nonverbal language of telepathic character and its basic vibration is love. A small child is present in this basic vibration of love that makes it impossible for it to differentiate itself from the whole. To this whole, belong mother, father, siblings, plants, animals, the earth, the sun, the universe. If a person has had a strong experience in which they became at one with the nature for a moment, for example, by watching a sunset, then they can get an impression of what a state of unity is. A child is constantly in this state of unity in the initial months of its lifetime.

Separation

From the soft spot on the top of the skull (reflector), it is possible to identify the child's direct energetic contact with its spiritual aura which gives it the feeling of unity. This contact is clearly visible right after birth. This contact is then gradually closed as the skull grows together and the soft spot on the child's skull becomes smaller and smaller. This does not mean that the child loses its spiritual contact but only that it becomes smaller, which is necessary if the child is to survive in the physical world. The child's next natural development of consciousness tends to be directed on learning to distinguish itself from the unity.

The child begins naturally now to turn its attention increasingly towards the physical world. It begins to focus on its hands, feet, father and mother to explore the difference between subject and object. This natural quest for light and consciousness cannot be seen, for example, in newborn mammals. This ability is something special only in humans.

When the child reaches an age of approximately two and a half - three years of age, it has learned the art of separation which has naturally been conveyed to it by the parents and its surroundings. It may now, through its newly acquired language, say "I want milk". It can now say "I" about itself and thereby separate subject from object. This humble form of "I" consciousness is like a ray of light that is born out of the unity state and is accumulated in the child's consciousness. The I-function of consciousness is like a burning lens that collects rays of light. This very function is like a gentle seed to be protected, watered, that needs to have heat, light and care in the right amount in order to grow big and strong. The function of "I" is related to the lower three chakras: the Root, the Hara and the Solar Plexus Chakras.

Further building of the "I"

The further building of "I" takes place through certain stages; the so-called seven-year period from 0 -7 - 14 - 21 - 28 - 35 - 42 – 49. After 49, a slow degradation of the self begins, which really starts physically from 25 years of age, though psychically it starts around the age of 49 years. The above mentioned period of seven years is very individual; it varies from person to person. Some people are ahead of others, some are several years behind. If anything is to be changed qualitatively in the consciousness form of "I", it usually has to be done within or around forty-nine years of age.

The higher astral energy field

The illustration shows the border area between the lower and higher astral aura.
The lower astral field is located below the hatched drawing,
the higher astral field is located above it.
The hatched part is an area where there are both lower and higher astral impulses.

The higher astral energy field and its function

The higher astral energy field brings, among other things, the person in emotional contact with his or her deeper character, self-consciousness and with higher emotions such as love, deep and true happiness, caring feelings, compassion, religious feelings, feeling of being connected with nature and the universe. A detailed characterisation of the human soul would be the higher astral field. Through these above mentioned feelings we associate ourselves with the world, nature and culture and they are the best innate tools that are available to us humans to bring harmony between different layers of consciousness in the energy field.

The above-mentioned deep and invigorating feelings are mostly unconsciously forming the foundation of what we basically believe in. May it be love for another person, devotion or faith in an ideal, etc.

The higher astral dimension is therefore also associated with angels and friendly spirits, whereas the lower astral dimension is often associated with the demonic, diabolical and with evil spirits. All these are obviously projections of a person good and bad qualities, where the negative qualities are projected in the lower astral and the positive ones in the higher astral, and obviously, it is only an illusion.

For us humans, it is essential to become aware of our fundamental higher astral feelings. These feelings are often associated with the concept of childhood faith. The kind of childhood faith we are talking about here has nothing to do with the child's naive world of imagination. What we are talking about here is one certain or more fundamental, specific higher feelings which have accompanied a person since their earliest childhood and therefore are perceived as timeless.

When a person has identified one or more specific higher emotions, he or she will be able to understand his or her deeper beliefs in a clearer perspective.

If a person believes in something that is not in harmony with these higher astral emotions, he or she will experience some form of deep frustration in his or her inner because that person did not appreciate those deeper feelings that have been there since his or her birth. It can go beyond the person's inner sense of self-confidence and feeling of authority and the person may encounter problems with authorities in the outer world. It is therefore very important for everyone to discover these deeper feelings so that each person can find his or her deeper and true beliefs.

Where it is written in the Bible that we must build our house on a rock, according to my view, this wants to tell us that we must form foundations of our beliefs, of our religious feelings according to these true deeper feelings. Then we will find what we really believe in, without interference from parents, society, religion or the head of the church. We will find access to our innate inner religion or spirituality.

The development and refinement of higher astral feelings will always be directed towards a deeper faith and the spiritual dimension, and thus, the innate spiritual qualities.

The lower astral aura

Instinctive emotional forces

From a higher consciousness perspective, there are no concepts like higher or lower. This type of view is connected to our everyday, common, awake state of consciousness, which often reacts in accordance to what we like and what we dislike. This special part of our consciousness is associated with the Solar Plexus Chakra and consciousness attitude in relation to sympathy and antipathy. This part of consciousness is often associated with animal instincts. Humans have used animal instincts through hundreds of thousands of years in order to survive and they are part of the entire human survival instinct.

Actually, all these so-called lower instincts are basically healthy and are part of natural human development. In normal children, who have had a reasonably healthy growth, all these instincts are accepted and they are healthy and intact. Parents transmit, consciously or unconsciously, their mental strengths and weaknesses to their child. Children copy the parent's psyche. It is necessary for them to learn to survive and children usually only have their parents as an example. If parents have a reasonable balance in the lower three chakras, this is automatically transferred to the child.

Therefore, an awareness and knowledge of what instincts represent emotionally, archetypally and psychologically, and how to develop them in the right direction and in the right way, is indisputably a necessity if we as people are to be able to make our own life and others' lives better in a spiritual sense. To transform our so-called lower character, it is necessary first of all to learn to accept and express them freely and easily without fear, before they can be finally transformed and released.

Usually, modern people do not have any deeper contact with these instincts in comparison to nature-bound people. It is possible to establish contact with the animal instincts, among other things, through night dreams in which animals appear. When natural instincts are suppressed, overly outlived, or come out of their natural balance, they are seeking a way inside to regain their natural balance. This compensating balancing takes place every night in most people's dream life, especially when people are too much centred in their head and have little connection to nature and their body. If this compensating, nightly balancing is not discovered and made conscious, a person ends up with frustration and a neurotic character of instinctual survival mechanisms. Throughout the various therapies, work with the body, meditation techniques and personal development methods, these movements in the unconscious can be made conscious.

When animal instincts come out of balance, they often become uncontrollable, dangerous and unpredictable. This frustrated state often leads to suffering in the world, in the form of wars, tragedies, cruelty, boundless lust, excessive selfishness, desire for power, envy, greed, gossip, slander, manipulation and many forms of diseases.

The lower part of human character is associated with instincts and emotional expression of the three lower chakras. If the instinctive emotional expression is not particularly conscious, it will often be out of natural control and therefore will seek to be made aware through regular self-expression and achieve natural control in that way. This means that if a person is unable to raise awareness of the instinctive emotional through ordinary human thought cognition, it must be experienced through the dark sides of the human race.

These dark sides are based on emotional and thought-related suppressive mechanisms and often involve an aspect of suffering. The inner unconscious suffering becomes visible through closer human relationships that a person has had and has.

A person's lower character is something that we have only started trying to understand in depth within the last hundred years. The concept of "shadow" in depth psychology should really be understood in depth, if we are to be successful in achieving relatively natural control of the instinctive emotional.

Lower character and the chakras

The lower human character is connected with instincts that are associated with the three lower chakras. These instincts have an emotional character that has to do with, for example, the following:

1. Instincts associated with the Root Chakra: the survival instinct, territory (nationality, clan and tribe). All contemporary and historical war conflicts, big and small, are mostly wars for land and territory and in this sense humans have much in common with animals. When these Root Chakra instincts become frustrated and out of natural control, they are often the cause of all war-like conflict in the world with the leitmotif of who has the highest right to conquer a land or territory, who owned the land first, etc.
2. Instincts associated with the Hara Chakra: sex power, which is reflected in sexual drive and the spread of genes and manifested in the form that is the natural expression of the sexual instinct. Human behaviour in the area of sex is

basically guided by our instincts that we also have in common with animals. It is an area that is heavily researched, and recent research shows that every tenth woman in a stable relationship becomes pregnant with a different man than her permanent male partner. For researchers, this indicates that sexual instinct in its effort to obtain the best genetic combination is stronger than expected.

This instinct is connected with survival of the species. Therefore, many more women than previously believed are naturally subject to this instinct in their sexual behaviour. Of course we can moralise in relation to adultery, but what do we know about what is natural and what is unnatural? Exaggerated or suppressed sexual behaviour, power struggles, rejection issues also belong among imbalances in relation with the Hara Chakra. After the survival instinct in the Root Chakra in relation to territory and land, sexual instinct is the one that has caused the biggest conflicts and wars in world history.

3. A power instinct that is reflected by the fact that we attempt to maximize power over our own lives is associated with the Solar Plexus Chakra.

The power instinct will always try to escape powerlessness – this applies to family, nationally and globally. The three lower chakras must be in balance if the power instinct is to develop in a healthy way. If there is an imbalance in the three lower chakras on a personal or national level, it will be reflected in the misuse of power against other people or nations.

The difference between emotions and feelings

The word 'emotion' often has a negative connotation in the alternative world that many people do not always understand. There is nothing wrong with emotion as such. Emotions are part of the reality we all live in. They are a part of life that makes it interesting, exciting and a source of knowledge.

The word emotion is used to describe the type of feelings that are associated with the Solar Plexus Chakra. There are many types of emotions such as anger, anxiety, grief, sympathy, joy, being hurt, enthusiasm, fervent infatuation, disappointment, helplessness, rejection, laughter, etc. It is decisive whether an emotion has a positive or negative impact on the consciousness and the energy field for how it is expressed. The balanced Solar Plexus Chakra is an expression of an emotional balance that is reflected in directly and honestly expressed emotions. When a person feels sorrow, anger, excitement, joy, etc., the direct expression emerges in the form of tears, healthy limit-setting anger, eruptions of joy, etc. When emotions are expressed in this way, they have a built-in direction to the heart and chest area where they come into contact with the higher astral field and with deeper feelings.

But when the emotional astral system is unbalanced, it is because of repressed, retained, stiffened and blocked emotions and feelings that are deposited as accumulated explosive energies in the astral system. When this type of negative emotions has been accumulated to an excessive degree, they can obtain a form of explosive and uncontrolled expression and often hurt the affected person and his or her loved ones.

Retained emotions can also be reflected in uncomfortable, heavy, thick unreleased moods that often occupy too much space of interpersonal relationships. They can destroy the good atmosphere at working places, in relationships, in family, etc. In the long term, this type of emotions is harmful. Therefore, when the word "emotional" is used in the alternative world, it is in connection with the latter type of emotion. The word 'feeling' is used to describe real deep feelings like love, compassion, deep joy, patience, faithfulness, indulgence, kindness, etc. True deep feelings are associated with the Heart Chakra and the higher astral field.

We are not accustomed to distinguishing feelings and emotions from each other. In relation to the energy field, the difference between emotion and feeling can be seen clearly, especially when emotions are suppressed. By observing the energy field in relation to suppressed emotions, we can see how the suppressed subtle and emotional energy dyes the astral and mental energy field. This emotional dyeing or influence of the astral and mental field reduces the supply of life energy in the etheric energy field, so vital organs of the physical body do not get the amount of vital energy they need. This is especially true for vital organs associated with the solar plexus area such as the liver, gall bladder, stomach, spleen, pancreas and intestines.

Emotions have an impact on the whole energy field and physical body in a positive way. It is characteristic of truly expressed emotions that they create wholeness and cooperation between all levels of the energy field and the physical body. Aurically, they create a whole person, whereas suppressed blocked emotions have a divisive, isolating effect. They block the higher part of the energy field. From an auric perspective, the task is obvious: how can one transform emotions into feelings?

Feelings and growth versus emotions and stagnation

From a personal development perspective, unilateral identification with emotions such as fear, anger, jealousy, greed, self-pity, sorrow, etc. leads to no growth. It leads to stagnation, because such an emotional identification is constantly repeating itself. It runs in circles. A person may keep on repeating these emotional patterns during a lifetime.

True feelings like love, true compassion, profound joy, self-knowledge and self-acceptance mean movement and growth of the whole person. We learn to appreciate ourselves and others through emotion. The difference between blocked emotions and true feelings is clearly defined in how we value life together with all the processes related to it. Blocked and stiffened emotions create stagnation in relation to life's direction and the natural growth associated with it. It is harder to appreciate life, oneself and other people, if it is like that.

If emotions are expressed honestly in life situations that trigger them, and in such a way that people you express them to are respected as fellow human beings and are not perceived as enemies, then the emotions themselves will seek a way to the hear and chest area and transform into feelings.

That is the way small children express their emotions. When they are sad or angry, they immediately give an expression to their emotions. Their spontaneous way of expressing themselves is what makes us adults think that they are so cute. If emotional expression becomes unnaturally retained in a child, its ability to transform emotions into feelings will gradually be altered. Then emotions will finally be expressed indirectly in a calculating way in which the child will want to achieve something specific by its way of expressing its emotions, thereby spontaneity of expression will also gradually disappear.

This way of expressing emotions excludes the possibility of transformation, since the expression of an emotion is driven by an underlying unconscious anxiety. The mode of expression is not free. The way to express yourself emotionally is held back and repressed by unconscious emotional ties which have a destructive impact on self-confidence, self-consciousness, self-esteem and belief in yourself and that in turn creates an experience of distrust and inferiority that leads compensatory to superiority and mistrust in relation to other people and the world.

Transformation of emotions

To transform emotions to the Heart Chakra requires a person to learn to appreciate him or herself, other people, nature and life itself. They cannot love others until they are able to love themself. They cannot appreciate others before they are not able to appreciate themself. So if they want to be loved, in reality they must first learn to love themself.

The reason of suppressed, stiffened and blocked emotions must be found. The cause must be re-experienced and felt. This is best achieved through therapy. Next, direct connection between emotion and expression must be strengthened and trained. Emotions have to be expressed honestly and in an appropriate way related to the particular situation. An honest way of expression means that a person really learns to feel what they have experienced emotionally before they expressed the emotion.

If emotions have been suppressed since childhood, a person has learned to express them in a negative pattern, which is not honest in its essence. Fear that binds free emotional expression can be of an autonomous nature and connected with the autonomic nervous system. Therefore, verbal expression has to be cleansed of impurities and destructive habitual behaviour. When a person feels, for example, jealousy, they have a tendency to accuse and blame the person who triggered it and that is not fair.

When an emotion is expressed in this way, a person is being dishonest. They lie to themselves and to whoever triggers the jealousy. If a person has such negative emotional patterns, they have to practice how to feel a particular emotion before it is expressed. They must learn to express an emotion as honestly and as accurately as possible, for example, by saying, "I am jealous and afraid of losing you." This applies to all types of emotions. In connection with the emotion of 'powerlessness', a person frequently reacts with aggression instead of expressing what is actually felt. In reality, they feel great grief and helplessness, but react with aggression. If they can become aware and conscious of these negative emotional expressions, it can be the beginning of the transformation of unbalanced emotions.

When an emotion is expressed honestly, it creates an entirely different reaction in the energy field. The person's expression is then true, which strengthens the life energy in the etheric energy field (see "The truth layer" on page 12). Through true expression a person creates an opening to the upper chakras, to their own higher astral field, and their higher mental and spiritual energy field. It is of great benefit if a person learns to express emotions honestly and sincerely. Hopefully it gives an energetic image of unbalanced emotional expression versus balanced emotional expression. A movement of emotional transformation can only be created in the energy field if emotions are expressed honestly and with respect for fellow humans.

If this is successful, slowly and surely a fertile ground for emotional transformation is created. Emotional energy will then move towards the Heart Chakra and the person will experience greater self-respect and thus greater appreciation of the self and the outside world because his or her emotional expression will be honest.

The person will begin to love him/herself, be at peace with him/herself, feel love for him/herself. This process will create harmony between all layers of consciousness in the energy field meaning a person will now experience trust, self-esteem and believe in him/herself, which in turn creates trust and faith in others, society, nature and the cosmos.

Importance of following a true feeling

If a person really has a strong feeling about or for something specific, they should follow that feeling. If it is a feeling and not an emotion, they should follow it, whatever that feeling requires of them. Spiritual growth means a feeling will add growth to human expression. It is the only true way a person can recognise themselves and their inner deeper individuality. It is the only true way to find oneself and to deal with that in relation to others and to the earth and the universe.

Sympathy and antipathy

Most people have certainly experienced that they like some people more than others, although they have never had any contact with them or talked to them. This feature relates to the astral energy field and is associated with the Solar Plexus Chakra and is called sympathy and antipathy. This special feature is a function related to our instincts, ability to make decisions and intuition. Sympathy and antipathy, or, likes and dislikes related to instincts are located in the lower astral aura, whereas the ability to make decisions and intuition are related to the higher astral field.

Instinctive sympathies and antipathies

Animals know what is dangerous by instinct. A rabbit knows that when it sees a fox, that this animal is synonymous with danger. Without this instinct or antipathy, it would not survive. From the shape and image of the fox, rabbits know genetically instinctively that they are in danger. This animal instinct is a part of their survival mechanism.

It is difficult in today's modern world for human survival instincts. Many people in the Western world have very poor contact with their healthy instincts. Real contact with them may even be deeply frightening to many people. Modern people feel alienated from their instinctive self and character. Throughout the nineties, many business leaders attended so-called courses of survival. The aim of these courses was to give people better contact with their basic instincts and thus better contact with their individual natural limits, which would automatically make someone a better leader-type.

Sympathy and antipathy are manifested in every human's life in the sense that there is something a person likes and something they dislike. It is, for example, reflected in our choice of clothes, food, furniture, home decorations, education, work and social surroundings. Sympathy and antipathy cover a wide area.

In the context of personal development it is important to be aware of a person's own sympathies and antipathies. If there are unconscious personality aspects in a person, they feel antipathy, and this unconscious antipathy steals energy because we project this unconscious part of ourselves onto others and we face a problem of seeing the negative in others and not noticing this aspect in ourselves. If we want to achieve further development, we must firstly be honest with ourselves. This means that if we have unacknowledged personality aspects, they must be discovered. Then they must be accepted.

Form of the astral energy field

Expansion and contraction

Most systems describe the astral energy field as egg- or pear-shaped. The astral energy field has a feature similar to that of the mental and spiritual field, that it can contract and expand. When, for example, we are scared and anxious, the astral energy field pulls together, it contracts. But when we are happy, feel love, feel comfort, are relaxed and have positive emotions in general, the astral energy field expands. People who have worked a lot with their emotions, and have transformed their fear and negative feelings felt toward themselves and other people, usually have a permanently expanded astral aura which can reach fifty cm from the physical body.

Talented performers such as actors, musicians, and the like, mainly use their astral field when they are on stage and performing. Their performance goes far beyond the stage and it means that their astral energy field expands during their performance to such an extent that it encompasses the entire hall. These are the magical moments when a performing artist merges with his or her audience and the audience cannot help but be deeply affected.

In very highly developed people the energy field can expand and spread enormously. In Arthur E. Powell's book "The Astral body", it is says, for example, that Buddha's aura is said to have been two kilometres around him.

The astral fire

Fire element
The fire element is associated with the astral energy field and the Solar Plexus Chakra. (See also the chapter related to archetypal symbols of the Solar Plexus Chakra.) Fire may, in its positive, building aspect, be warming and controlled, as we, for example, see it symbolically in a fireplace, a burning candle or a campfire, etc. In its negative, destructive aspect, fire is uncontrollable and destructive. For example, symbolically it can be seen in burning houses and buildings, cities and nature. Fire, in this case, is consuming and destructive, while in its positive aspect, as mentioned above, it is warming and controlled. Fire symbolises man's astral consciousness form.

Physically, the fire element is expressed through burning of energy, through the digestive process and through the fact that the human body is kept in normal function at about 37 degrees of Celsius. Psychologically, in its positive aspect, the fire element is expressed through engagement and enthusiasm, human warmth and humour, righteous limit-setting anger, etc. Negatively, it comes to be expressed as emotional coldness, excessive enthusiasm, mental inflation, fever, and strong heat radiating around the head.

The astral inner fire will behave positively, if a person is true and consistent with him/herself. It becomes negative if a person is false and goes against his/her deeper character or treats it badly. If a person goes against his deeper character, it undermines his/her ethics and morality. If this is happening for a longer period of time, finally the affected person loses the feeling for what is untrue, what is true and true for him/herself. Such a person is easily subjected to negative aspects of the astral fire.

Destructive fire of inflation
When a person has difficulty in deciding what feels authentic and what inauthentic, he or she will often be tempted to let the outer authorities' opinions and attitudes dominate him or her. It can go so far as the person thinking those attitudes and opinions are something that he or she has formed.

When it comes to this situation, this is a person who has fallen victim to inflation. Inflation means that the ego (the lower astral and the lower mental awareness aspects) steals from what rightfully belongs to the collective, higher spiritual communities. This means that the human ego identifies itself with something that it is not, even existentially. The ego places itself on a higher position than where it originally and authentically belongs.

This side of human nature is embodied in Greek mythology, in the myth of Daedalus and his son Icarus. Daedalus built a labyrinth on Crete. The difficulty was not to enter the labyrinth but to get out of it again, after reaching its centre.

Human labyrinth of thoughts is diverse. A person can get stuck in his/her limitations that he/she may have created (labyrinth). In the context of inflation, the limit lies in people identifying with ideas they do not have existentially any contact with and hence, no real experience with and thus, there is no real deeper basis to identify them with. Inflation is often the real cause of personal limitations, which is extremely appropriate for many people nowadays, without them really understanding why.

What does a person do then? How to find a way back to their inner self? How to get rid of false identifications? The danger of inflation is always present here. A person in such a situation could easily be tempted. Daedalus and Icarus were trapped in their own labyrinth and in order to escape from it they created wings and learned to fly. They learned that consciousness can uplift or transcend personality beyond its limitations.

In his excessive enthusiasm (inflation), Icarus flew so high that he came too close to the sun and the wax of his wings melted and he fell into the sea and drowned. Symbolically it means that the flames of inflation consumed him from inside and destroyed his natural contact with his consciousness and thus to his real and true personality.

On a more everyday basis, inflation is also reflected in economy and it is known to many people. From the mid-nineties until 2002, we might have witnessed a phenomenon in the IT industry that was also marked by aspects of inflation. Enthusiasm for the stock markets for the IT industry meant that initially IT shares rose gradually until they reached the point where all realism disappeared. Suddenly, the shares fell drastically. The result being that many people lost large amounts of money, their savings they had invested in IT shares and many small IT companies went bankrupt. I mention this example because economy and inflation are inseparable. People with an inflated inflation-like personality will initially usurp power (money) from society. When society finds out that the inflated person is untrustworthy, that person loses all energy inputs and will be thrown back into reality, often with large financial losses and deep debts. It is beneficial to pay attention when coping with the destructive, consuming inner fire of inflation.

The danger of inflation

All inflation is dangerous because the ego cannot separate itself from the source of inflation and because it cannot be cured from the outside. It is only the ego itself that may quit from external or internal sources of power. If an inflated person is not stopped by his or her own force, the inner astral fire will consume and undermine his or her personality even more, which of course is deeply tragic in human terms.

Healing of inflation

If an inflated person wishes to come back to his/her real and true self, he/she must learn to separate himself or herself from the power source and discover the underlying emotional cause of inflation. It can be painful and full of suffering. But this pain and suffering is part of the healing process associated with an inflated person.

Another aspect of the healing process is that the inflated person finds a way back down to earth. All daily activities will be fully respected again; may it be economy, work, family, cleaning, healthy cooking and shopping. It is usually all these everyday activities inflated people feel superior to.

Four astral gates

Tibetan Mandala illustrating the four astral gates

The astral dimension expresses itself in feelings and emotions. Feelings are related to the higher astral field, emotions are related to the lower astral field. The so-called evil and bad energies are related to the lower human astral area. Since time immemorial, people have protected themselves against the so-called evil spirits through various rites of religious character that should have kept the evil spirits or bad energy away. In this context, it is naturally important to be aware of a person's own possible projection and suppression mechanisms.

The character of such ceremonies varies from culture to culture, but there is a characteristic feature in all of them. Almost all protection rituals work with the four cardinal directions.

On the Mandala illustration at the top of the page, four entrances or gates to the inner part of the Mandala can be seen in the outer circle. Each gate is guarded or protected by a symbolic guardian or holy incantation.

If a person being in an expanded state of consciousness reaches the psychic territory where personality begins to dissolve into higher consciousness, this person encounters anxiety of death reflected in four different types of fear: the fear of dying, fear of going mad, fear to get a terminal illness and the fear of deeper sexuality. These are the four basic forms of collective unconscious fear that protect the personality and the "I" to be dissolved in an expanded state of consciousness.

Should a person cross this deep inner boundary, for example, during meditation, he or she must have been going through a process of preparation for several years until they had achieved a relatively good balance of the chakra system. The ordinary consciousness must pass these four internal border gates, if it wants to meet the fifth, sixth and seventh level of consciousness at its inner.

Guardians of the threshold

In depth psychology, these deep psychological boundary mechanisms are called "threshold guardians". It is the limit for general consciousness. Once the general consciousness comes into contact with this deep area, it may end up meeting the demonic, collective unconscious fear of death and is often scared to death. Many young people who have experimented with psychedelic drugs have, without realising it, encountered these "threshold guardians" with the result being that they became psychotic. It requires long preparation and existential balance if a person is to be mentally able to meet the threshold guardians. In most fairy tales, only the hero who conquers the monstrous demonic forces and gets through to the treasure, to the princess, gets half of the kingdom. In the Mandala illustration, it is these forces which guard the four gates. General awareness meets all the inner anxiety in all its forms and manifestations at these gates.

Expert advice

It is only through expert advice and guidance from someone who already knows the way, or by God's grace, that it is possible for an unprepared and untrained person to cross this border. It is not something that a man should be exposed to without appropriate preparation and expert guidance from a skilled advisor or teacher.

If a person gets through to these higher realms of consciousness without preparation and without existential necessary ethics, then suddenly spiritual light will be pouring into the personality. If there are any imbalances in the personality, the spiritual light will flow in the direction of these imbalances and light them through, illuminating them with such power that the personality would only be able to perceive and feel these imbalances, and often it is a psychological hell. If that happens, the affected personality's only wish is that the inner hell disappears as soon as possible, because such terrible conditions can bring people close to or into psychotic states.

Therefore, guidance from a spiritual teacher, who already knows the way, is of great importance if such an internal meeting with the higher consciousness is to be successful.

Cleansing of space and aura

In relation to cleansing and transforming energy in a room that has a bad atmosphere, the four cardinal directions can be used. Here is a description of how it can be done:

1. Stand in the middle of the room facing the corner that is closest to north. Imagine, that through a deep breath, you inhale all the bad energy from the north corner and visualise black colour. During exhalation you visualise white light, breathing out in the direction of the north corner.
2. Then turn right, facing the east corner. There you repeat the same action with breathing and visualisation as you did in the north corner.
3. Turn right towards the south corner and repeat the very same action.
4. Turn right, facing the west corner and repeat the same action again.

Then the room is cleansed of bad energy and this technique is complete. Afterwards, a person can possibly cleanse their own aura. This is done in a standing position by visualising light on a point approximately 30 cm above the head and letting this light fill all areas of the energy field. They start at the top and finish in a point approximately 30 cm below the feet.

This exercise is then finished. If a person has had body contact with other people through the whole day, then they might cleanse their aura by taking a shower for at least five minutes. On our courses, other techniques of how to cleanse the energy field are also presented.

Astral consciousness - astral travel - astral projection

Detachment of consciousness
In its higher aspects, consciousness is not bound to the body. If consciousness identifies itself fully with physical reality, it cannot get a separated experience of the astral reality. In this case, it only usually happens in the case of shock, accident or similar incidents.

I am certain that a very large number of people have experienced their consciousness outside their body. Personally, I know some people who have experienced being out of their body for longer or shorter times. In addition, there is also my own experience.

Children and out-of-body experience
It is far more common that children can separate their consciousness from the physical and etheric dimension. Some years ago my daughter told me of the time she was a child and travelled around our house and garden when she slept or rested. I asked what she meant, and she explained to me that she often felt, when she rested or were about to fall asleep, that her hands began to tingle as if they were numb or like when you have a fever. When this happened, she knew that she would fly. She explained that she flew around various rooms of the house and through the garden. She said she always stayed within those limits. She had these experiences between 5 to 9 years of age and that was all she consciously remembered.

Another good example of children's approach to astral dimension is the story of my former neighbours. They were a couple with a two-year-old child. The man could consciously leave his physical body. When he was away from home physically and spent the night elsewhere, he travelled home to his wife and child in the astral dimension. His child discovered his father's astral presence and waved and called out to him. Again, it is very common for small children to experience and see the astral dimension.

I am certain that many parents have heard their children telling similar stories when they were already older. When children are in the above-mentioned age, they very rarely tell their parents about such experiences. Intuitively, they know that they will not be understood.

From my own childhoo, I especially remember when I was on the borderline between being in my body and being outside it. When I was in this state, I could not consciously move my body and my perception of distance was distorted. I could see my breath as a cosmic bellows which was as large as the entire universe, or I had the feeling that the distance from my eyes down to my feet was several kilometres long.

Experiences involving the feeling of pins and needles in your hands, the feeling of fever, great distortion of distance and size are associated with the astral energy field and astral consciousness dimension. The usual boundary separating consciousness dissolves into the astral consciousness form where it lets go of its normal physical way of thinking and slips into a state that is limited only by ideas that are of physical character. A good example of this was provided by Bob Moore during one of his courses. When he first deliberately left his physical body, he was on the first floor of his parents' house. He wanted to be in a room downstairs and thus floated down the stairs, grabbed the door handle and was immediately back in his physical body. When you think physically, you become physical.

Adults and out of body experience

When we become adults, in our awareness we become accustomed to reality only being of a physical nature. The world is as we believe it is. Consciousness of most adults is more or less closed. With closed I mean that the possibility of multiple realities existing maybe simultaneously, is not present in the consciousness. Consciousness is cemented in fixed opinions and solid material of the Root Chakra. There is nothing wrong with it if a person allows others to have a different opinion.

It is widely known that people who have had an accident, undergone surgery or similar shock events frequently report that they were consciously present during their resuscitation or surgery. They could then retell exactly what was said, though during those circumstances they had been deeply unconscious. This kind of out-of-body experience is associated with shock and deeply traumatic experiences. After this type of experience, it can often take time to get into the body again. A person can have a constant feeling of walking beside themselves, or to have a feeling they are not really themself. In this context, it is good to undergo thought field therapy. Thought field therapy is a technique where the person who heals very easily taps on the body of the recipient. This is done all over the body. You start from the top and finish down at the feet.

When an adult experiences that his or her consciousness is outside their body, they are deeply relaxed. I have an acquaintance who attended a Nidra Yoga course. Nidra Yoga is a very deep relaxation method that originates from India where each body part is consciously relaxed and this procedure is supported by instructions from a teacher. The person I know experienced that during exercises she could suddenly look down at her body and it frightened her a lot. This experience immediately brought her back into physical reality, she rose and thereafter she never practised Nidra Yoga again. This is a pity.

Personally, I think that we should make people who are doing deep relaxation exercises aware that there is a chance they can experience their consciousness outside the body if they become deeply relaxed. If they had this information and were also taught how to behave when they were outside the body, nothing similar to my acquaintance's experience would happen to them.

Lucid consciousness

Lucid means luminous. Lucid consciousness means that the consciousness is more transparent to itself. Consciousness has an awakened contact with areas beyond the norm and that means that a person can also be consciously awake in a dream state.

A person who develops his astral consciousness undergoes some preliminary stages before he or she can consciously leave the body. These preliminary stages occur when the person is deeply relaxed, or when the person is dreaming some very specific dreams. The person may also discover a tingling sensation in their hands or body. Or the person may be aware that he or she is in bed at home while he or she dreams of being somewhere else in the world. Such alertness in dreams indicates that an awakening is taking place in the consciousness in relation to the astral dimension. The awareness then begins to have a choice. It can either choose whether to indulge itself in the lucid awake state of consciousness in the dream or whether it wants to dream in the average way.

Most people who come so far choose the first state. The adult consciousness begins to work on getting in touch with the open state of consciousness he or she had access to as a child, but this time consciousness is much more creative. For instance, it has dreams of flying when it is flying in an acrobatic way in the air with a wonderful feeling of freedom while it knows that its body lies in bed.

In the next phase, the consciousness begins to control lucid dreams. It decides what the dream should be about and how it should end. This is the transition to an out of body experience. In what follows, the out-of-body experience is going to be referred to in an abridged form of OOBE. Here is some advice that should be followed.

Advice

1. People who are not thoroughly prepared for an OOBE may become emotionally overwhelmed and very scared when they leave their physical body. This negative experience can implant itself as a traumatic death and life anxiety.
2. People with anxiety phobias or other mental imbalances should not, under any circumstances, experiment with OOBE. This also applies to people who are more or less anxious. Before starting to experiment with OOBE, a person should get a grip on their anxieties, make themselves aware of them and process them.

OOBE and the energy field

What we call astral travel, astral projection or out-of-body experience, takes place in the way that the astral, mental and spiritual aura frees itself from the physical body. You do not just leave the physical body with the astral energy field but also the rest of one's superordinate awareness, the mental and spiritual aura also accompanies this journey.

Why OOBE is called astral travel and astral projection
It is called astral travel or astral projection because the consciousness of most people is centred in the astral dimension during an OOBE. A person can discover where their consciousness is centred during an OOBE.

Different stages of consciousness of OOBE
For most cases of OOBE, consciousness is dreamlike but awake and lucid. The reality you are in during an OOBE is not as clear as when you are centred in an awake, daily conscious state. When reality is experienced in an OOBE in this way, consciousness is centred in the astral dimension, which is most common in the case of most astral travels.

If the reality that a person experiences in an OOBE is as clear as the daily, awake conscious state, consciousness is centred in the astral and mental dimension.

If the reality in an OOBE is clearer and more real than the normal daily, awake consciousness, consciousness is centred in the astral, mental and spiritual dimension.

It might happen that in an OOBE you can simultaneously be in more than one consciousness dimension. You can experience consciousness, scenes or scenery in an OOBE as dreamy, foggy and cloudy, thus energy and intensity increases and become clearer and more daily consciousness-like impressions. From there, in a few rare cases, consciousness can switch to a higher, more intense clarity and light; from there the normal awake state appears to be dreamlike and unreal.

Shamanic state of consciousness
Since the earliest times, man has known a way to be able to liberate consciousness from the body. This property has been used by tribal medicine men or shamans to establish contact with spirits so they could provide guidance in relation to disease and important decisions. The applied technique, which some nature-bound people and nations still use, is the following: the body is brought into an ecstatic dance, the medicine man or shaman uses holy narcotic mushrooms and plays monotonously on his handmade drum.

Such technique enables the medicine man or shaman to be able to leave their physical body and get help and guidance from the world of spirits as they need them.

The astral energy field and music

Music has an enormous significance in our modern world. Just a hundred years ago, music was accessible to only very few people. Today, most people have access to music and that has to be considered as an advantage, especially if music is used with care and consideration. When I say with care and consideration, it is because music affects the astral energy field very strongly.

Music can be compared to an expression of human emotions and feelings in tone and sound. When this language of tone and sound reaches our ears, mind and body, we are affected by the feelings and emotions that are present in the music, whether we like it or not. Emotions and feelings of music have such property that they form astral landscapes, or, expressed in another way, music builds inner images. These inner images differ from person to person, but if we examine them, we will discover that they contain the same archetypal basic forms significant for the majority of people who listen to a particular piece of music. In my courses, I have used my own compositions and music of other composers, from which I studied the image building power of music in many attendees of my courses. By observing the individual symbols that were most energy charged, a common theme from these symbols could be deduced connected to one or more archetypes.

Through auric sight, it is possible to see the direct effect of music on the energy field. Music can evoke certain emotions and colours, create good or bad polarity, create specific geometric structures that the listener brings into his or her inner or leads them out of him or herself. The effect of music is diverse.

In connection with the astral energy field and personal development, it is good to listen to music that can harmonise and bring well-being and deep relaxation into the energy field, consciousness and body. A person should do this once a day, if possible. The music used should be something that will bring the desired effect.

If you are unsure about which music has the desired effect, you should experiment. I would recommend my own compositions if you are still uncertain about the choice of music to use. I know the impact that my music has on myself and on many other people, so I can highly recommend it to anyone. See page 185 for more details.

Astral colours

About astral colours in general

All colours, consciously or unconsciously, have an emotional resonance in human consciousness. Probably a lot of people would agree. Therefore, a colour is not just a visual experience. It is also an emotional experience. Colour perception, however, varies from person to person depending on what people associate with colours psychologically. If we have a visual view on colours without any personal association and without interference of our own experienced psychic content, colours then create emotional states of consciousness that are energetically and aurically very similar in all humans.

It is these colours that we call the astral colours because emotional feeling-based states dye, add colour to, consciousness that is then reflected into the energy field as radiation and energetically and aurically it is experienced as colours.

As far as feelings and emotions are concerned, they are always in motion and are very rarely static. It is important the reader is aware that the illustrations of colours in the book are frozen images of a still developing spiral-like psychological and emotional movement in an either negative or positive direction. Colours seen as states of consciousness develop more or less constantly. Astral colours can be expressed in three categories:

1. Harmful astral colours
2. Normal astral colours
3. Higher astral colours

One of the areas of human consciousness where little movement and development occurs, can be observed in connection with unconscious repression of emotions. This area of consciousness is called the lower astral field and is related to the Solar Plexus Chakra.

Harmful astral colours

Lower astral colours are manifested in connection with various types of unconscious, repressed or too excessively outlived emotional states of mind which dye the astral energy field through their mood and atmosphere. These types of emotional states of mind are an expression of higher or lower degrees of emotional imbalance and are manifested as specific colours and symbols in the astral energy field. We call these colours and symbols harmful, since in the long term they lead to diseases. The energetic subtle colour radiance of these unbalanced, disease-causing emotional states manifests itself as impure, dull and unclear colours in the energy field.

Harmful emotional colours can be recognised in the astral energy field or in a person's night dreams. They tend to influence or dye the etheric energy field that is closest to the surface of the skin. A person's "here and now" situation is reflected in this etheric layer which we call the layer of presence and manifestation.

This particular type of emotionally based dull, impure colour tends to reduce the "flow" or free movement of life energy in the etheric energy field, which then cannot deliver necessary vital energy to various body organs. Therefore, a person should be aware of them and be careful. The following passage describes the negative, harmful emotional colours. One more thing should be mentioned. Emotions and feelings that cannot be expressed in a normal manner tend to be deposited as light blue shades on the lower body and legs. The light blue, ice blue colour in these areas, is associated with repression and suppression mechanisms and has nothing to do with healing. It is a sign of those emotions not being able to be expressed but are instead suppressed and are directed by the Throat Chakra.

Brown – colour of stagnation

Aurically, brown is a mixture of orange and black in the astral energy field. Orange is a health and well-being colour. When people have a deeply selfish, egoistic motif, maybe consciously or unconsciously, this motif expresses itself as a black colour blending with the orange healing colour. This colour combination creates a brown shade in the energy field, which obviously has a harmful effect on the etheric life energy which is reduced by it.

There is healthy and unhealthy egoism. The necessary natural health protective, limited egoism or selfishness has a deep orange colour whereas unhealthy egoism is brown. What creates the difference between healthy and unhealthy egotism, is the underlying motif. Often unconscious stagnating emotional states are the power drive behind many kinds of unhealthy egoism. This unhealthy egoism has a harmful effect on the person's own energy system which is expressed as shades of brown. The darker shades of brown, the stronger it the stagnating unconscious emotional motif.

Aurically, unhealthy egoism seems to have an isolating effect on the energy field.

This means that unhealthy egoism is not in harmony with the rest of the energy system. The darker the brown is, the more isolation exists.

These emotional stagnations are reflected in the astral energy field and in night dreams as brown shades. When there is a positive change in connection with the emotional expression, brown first turns into a dark beige shade. In the context of a healing process, positive change in emotional expressions results in a change of brown, so that it gradually becomes lighter. First, a dark beige shade appears, then beige and light beige. Beige means that there has been a movement in the stagnating emotional energy of a person's verbal emotional expression. It means that the life energy, especially in connection with the Solar Plexus and the Hara Chakra, can flow freely again and thereby provide the Solar Plexus and Hara Chakra with life energy that these chakras with their corresponding vital organs need. When the natural balance is restored, beige shades turn into orange, crocus-like yellow and yellow. These colours indicate that there has been more balance established in the part of the energy system associated with the Solar Plexus and Hara Chakra.

Grey-brown shades

When there are grey-brown shades observed in the astral energy field or in night dreams, this refers to the emotion of greed or relative emotions such as lust, excessive possessiveness, greediness, etc. Greed is basically a spiritual disease.

These emotions often have an underlying common theme - the "rejection problem". I can mention an example of a man who suffered from almost pathological greed. I have worked with this man on this unbalanced emotion in all its different depths and regressively we ended in the fetal phase of development, in which the affected person did not experience being nourished enough and therefore he was in a constant state of hunger. The fetus had experienced this first constant state of hunger as rejection of its existence that later developed into a fear of "not getting enough". This fear was of course rejected by his older siblings and parents with the result that he never felt his needs were met adequately - as a child and later as an adult. Since awareness of this emotion has been made, he could finally begin to get rid of his fears of being "rejected" and "not getting enough".

Grey-green shades

Grey-green shades are often seen in terms of stress. Two people can do exactly the same job, but only one gets stressed by it. Stress is often caused by underlying unconscious and unprocessed emotions, which are provoked when a person feels under pressure.

Stress is one of the major causes of illnesses in our times. A human being is far more resistant to stress, if the underlying unconscious emotions are acknowledged and processed. I do not mean that people should let themselves be abused in their professional life by society or to be voluntarily put under stress until they are totally devastated by it. I think it is a sort of vicious circle that people are more and more pushed to compete to be able to stand the competitive fight. Such a lifestyle supported by society is bad in the long term from an economical point of view, though in the short term it pays off. The bill for such a sick attitude legalised by our society comes later.

A human being is far better equipped against stress and disease, and adapts to burdens connected with the job market, if the underlying unconscious emotions are processed and acknowledged.

The grey-green shades are often seen in the mental etheric field as mental stress. Thoughts cannot calm down, their speed is too high. It is difficult to charge up again, resulting in difficulty getting to sleep. It is as if we were in a vicious circle that is hard to get out of again. This is perfectly characterised by grey-green shades.

The underlying motif of many forms of stress is absorption. One becomes totally abs The underlying motif of many forms of stress is absorption. You become totally absorbed in your work, project or goal, so you forget or repress the contact to your own deeper character. This will cause long term stress when the ordinary consciousness cannot fall back into itself, cannot rest in itself, nor can be itself.

The reason that a man lets himself be absorbed often has a deeper emotional motif that can often (but not always) be related to a lack of acceptance and love in early childhood. The child has experienced that if it wanted to be loved and accepted, it had to wear a mask and play a certain role. First, the child was denied acceptance and love by being who it was. Then, more and more, it has been pushed to play a role in order to achieve acceptance and love.

When people let themselves get under pressure and have stress in the job market, it is often because they become absorbed in this old emotional pattern of behaviour from their childhood. By raising an awareness of the reason why a person puts stress onto themselves and becomes absorbed when under pressure, the fear of not being accepted and loved as one can finally be released and dissolved. When this anxiety is released, the person can do the same job without getting stressed.

Yellow-green shades

Yellow-green shades in the astral energy field and dreams can be an expression of envy, jealousy or false growth. Green colour is usually a growth colour associated with the Heart Chakra and balance, but here the yellow-green colour is a combination of the yellow Solar Plexus Chakra colour and black. Black colour is here an expression of unawareness. When black is aurically mixed with yellow, the resulting shade is yellow-green. This colour can best be compared to the colour of rotten yellow-green algae in still waters.

The yellow-green colour is reflected in the energy field when people are overshadowed by "the fear of losing" in connection with envy – we even say: to be green with envy. This colour is also possible to observe in the energy field in relation to false growth and disease.

The motif is often "rejection" which is found both in the grey-brown and grey-green shade, but in this case it is connected with "inferiority".

The reason for this type of inferiority and rejection issues can often (but not always) be found in early childhood. Individuals with these problems or challenges have often experienced failure associated with their underlying basic needs. The reason may, for example, be that the child has not had adequate body contact, closeness and human warmth, that it would have needed. Or it might have experienced the adults not having time for it, that it was rather taken for a troublemaker than for a welcome child. Maybe it had to fall asleep many times crying. It is also possible that the child was immediately taken away or separated from its mother after the umbilical cord was cut and today this is strongly discouraged. The child should first be put on the mother's belly before the umbilical cord is cut. For some babies, it can be a traumatic experience being separated from their mother shortly after they came out of the birth canal. Such an experience can be deposited as shock in the astral system and the child might feel this separation as rejection from its mother's side.

Red-brown shades

Emotions such as hatred, blind rage, uncontrolled rage and similar related emotions that are regularly experienced, can be observed as red-brown shades in the astral energy field. These kinds of unbalanced emotion have a volcano-like character. They explode in regular intervals to reduce the pressure of the suppressed content in the person's astral energy system. The person's emotional system is like a steam boiler under pressure. When the pressure gets too high, excessive pressure is released through uncontrolled violent emotions of aggressive character.

If a person has this kind of emotional behaviour, it is possible to work with it and change it. The person can start by registering time intervals between the inappropriate emotional outbreaks by marking them in a calendar. From this record, it is possible to predict when the next outbreak occurs, because these types of emotion are built up and released in the astral energy field on a regular basis. By looking at time intervals between the outbreaks, we can identify the intervals between emotional outbursts. This kind of awareness can create a desire to gain more control over a person's emotional system. It is possible to find a constructive way to reduce pressure of the emotional system. It can be by means of sports, fitness, training and other such activities.

The actual cause of the destructive emotional outbreaks often has a connection to the Hara Chakra, where early experiences in childhood, for instance, of great "powerlessness", may have led to a destructive behaviour of uncontrolled anger directed on the outside environment. This threatening and often destructive anger arises in a compensatory way in order to to get away from the powerlessness and to gain power over the situation, so it can be controlled by the affected person. Thereby, the person is trying, consciously or unconsciously, to control and manipulate his or her environment. The inner fear of "pow erlessness" is projected here onto the surroundings and in certain emotional situations it can feel like a threat. The feeling of powerlessness in childhood can result in deep mistrust towards all forms of authorities, society, world, father or mother and also a fear of powerlessness that the affected person's adult life turns into emotional affection. This kind of anxiety can be an underlying drive of power to achieve as much power over one's life as possible. In its more controlled form, the person attempts to secure him or herself in all possible areas of life that can give him or her a sense of power over powerlessness and it may be in economic, family and social contexts. It may also be in the form of control over their own body.

Through awareness of this disorder a person will find that he or she achieves an even more natural control over his/her emotional system. One way to achieve greater emotional control is through breathing exercises. Many people with this type of anxiety are unconsciously trying to gain control over it by activities which often are of a physical character but which may also be of a psychological character. Through their demanding sport activities, usually at the amateur level, they unconsciously use their breathing function to achieve a form of control. At the same time, such an activity is an unconscious desire to achieve control. It provides a kind of security, while the lung function contributes to creating a natural control over the emotional system.

By performing a specific breathing exercise consciously for about 10 minutes a day, one can achieve the same feeling of control and while doing this exercise unconscious material can be brought to consciousness. This breathing exercise is a basic exercise in personal development. It takes place between the Pineal Chakra and the Hara Chakra.

Grey

I call the colour grey "the inner straitjacket". Grey is a shade that can be seen with the onset of depression, by excessive abuse of alcohol, by smoking of tobacco. When a person is moving into a depressive state, he or she sees and experiences everything as grey. In the astral energy field, everything is reflected as grey, the accompanying feeling is "isolation and confinement". The person is trapped in his or her own emotional trap that he/she feels unable to escape from. The person feels trapped, imprisoned or chained. This feeling of "being bound" creates grey shades in the astral energy field. The darker the grey, the bigger the feeling of isolation is. Once the colour becomes so dark that it is almost black, the person's is in a time of depression's culmination.

In relation to tobacco smoking, and the like, a greyish coloration of the astral and etheric field can be observed in the heart and chest area reducing the "flow" of the life energy in this area. This greyish mist dissolves approximately 45 minutes after the completion of smoking. It is definitely unhealthy to smoke from the auric energetic point of view, too.

It is often difficult for people who feel, for one reason or another, "inner confinedness". If the cause of this often unconscious feeling of "being confined" is not acknowledged, people affected by this emotion will unconsciously seek out such life situations where the feeling of "being imprisoned – being chained" is amplified. The purpose of such behaviour is basically a desire to be conscious of the reason of this dominant feeling. In its mild form, this emotion can create feelings of "being isolated and lonely" in different contexts of relationships, professional and social matters. In its strongest form, people actually commit crime from an unconscious desire to be imprisoned or isolated physically.

The underlying cause of this fundamental sense of isolation must again be found in childhood and in special experiences in connection with birth. Many children have often experienced a form of punishment of being sent to their rooms, locked up or even were grounded. Many children consider this form of exclusion and isolation as incomprehensible. From the reaction and response of its environment, the child understands that it has been naughty, but without understanding what was so rude in its behaviour. The child simply does not understand why it must be punished. If this pattern of parental behaviour is repeated sufficiently enough, the child begins to behave naughtily. It seeks unconsciously a reasonable explanation to why it is being punished. It is one of the areas where parents should be very careful with their form of punishment. They must really be sure that the child understands why it is being punished. Parents should also be very careful not to transmit their anxiety onto their child. Anxiety is often, "the fear of being disgraced".

Another reason for this kind of emotion can be found in birth. If a yet unborn baby was stuck helplessly in the birth canal for a long time, we can relate this to growing up and getting into various forms of "being bound, feeling like you are an inner prison or a feeling that there is no way out of a life situation". According to Stanislav Grof, it is the third birth matrix out of four, where the key words are: "no way out".

The third reason for this unbalanced emotion may be that children in early childhood, from the age of six months until they are two or three years old, have been placed in their pram with too many clothes on, so they could not move and experienced an uncomfortable warmth. Although they had been crying and giving an expression of their dissatisfaction with that situation, they had purposely been fully ignored. The child does not understand this kind of abuse. It is unnatural for it. Often it can also be punished by being fixed into a harness, so even more it is not possible to get free. It feels fixed and imprisoned.

In the former Soviet Union, there was a special pedagogical approach practised: small children were fixed in their prams so that it was impossible for them to move and people were convinced that in this way they would be brought up to be better citizens of the country.

Fear may, in its extreme form, be reflected as claustrophobia, which the person unconsciously seeks out or feels attracted to in order to become aware of the reason of his or her anxiety. There is obviously a great deal of helplessness behind this harmful emotion, but the behaviour is often the opposite of the red-brown shade of "powerlessness" that tries to free itself by applying violence and power. The grey form of behaviour is often the quiet, accepting, the not demanding behaviour, in which the person can withdraw to a place in his or her consciousness that has a certain resemblance to an inner psychic prison. Breathing exercise between the Pineal Chakra and the Hara Chakra can be helpful with this problem.

Black

Black or darkness is often an expression of a lack of awareness of an emotional underlying hidden motif such as depression, a great change or death. But black can also mean protection. The colour black in the astral energy field and dreams may indicate the above-mentioned phenomena.

Lack of awareness and black

A person's so-called dark sides are often lying in unconsciousness and darkness. A deep lack of awareness of a person's own negative emotions creates darkness and explosive events in life. If they do not want to acknowledge it, life itself must be the teacher for such a person. The greatest anxiety and main dark side or shadow is death, fear of death or fear of life.

Depression and black

A constant fear of life can lead to depression. When depression culminates, all light and hope are extinguished. This darkness can be seen in the energy field as widespread black or a darkening of consciousness. The condition is often compared to Christ on the cross, where he called in deep despair: "My God, my God, why hast thou forsaken me?" This deeply depressive state is also called "Dark night of the soul". When a person is in the deepest darkness, the light is closest to him or her. If a person finds the light (the person's own light of soul) in the darkness, he or she has overcome fear of life and death. Thus the depression was positive and it is often followed by a changed attitude to life and major changes in life. However, if a person cannot overcome his fear of life and is unable to find the light in him or herself, it can lead to his or her spiritual or physical death.

Protection and black

In the Western Protestant world, priests wear black during their masses. In the Islamic world, there are places where women wear only black clothes. Black colour can be seen in connection with changes around the Heart Chakra. It is reflected in the black colour of the Yin & Yang symbol that is usually located in the Heart Chakra. The dark or black here symbolises the ancient darkness or uncreated light; the uncreated light that exists in darkness before all creation. In the Bible it is written: And God said: "Let there be light and there was light". This light was created and sent out from the ancient darkness or it was idling in the ancient darkness. The ancient darkness is the symbol of the universal womb from which all light originates. People who experience meditative silence can encounter the ancient darkness or the uncreated light.

In this source of all consciousness of existence, the human consciousness reaches back to its source – to its origin and source. This source of human consciousness contains both light and darkness. There is no difference between the light and the darkness. Consciousness is both the passive, receiving universal feminine primordial energy (darkness) and also the active, handling and creative masculine energy (light).

Perhaps it is this deep archetypal metaphor that forms the basis for people dressing in black in connection with ritual and religious activities.

Normal astral colours
in connection to personality development

With regards to personal development, the colours red, orange and yellow are in particular included, but of course also the colours of the upper chakras. When these colours are clean in the astral energy field, it indicates existential emotional balance in the person's contact with the Root, Hara and Solar Plexus Chakras and also indicates a good contact with the Heart Chakra and the rest of the upper chakras. There can be no real balancing of the lower chakras going on without the involvement of the Heart Chakra and the self-recognition ability. The Heart Chakra is the point of balance in man. Should there be a personal development of the three lower chakras, the Heart Chakra must be involved.

Red
Red is the most active colour in the entire energy system. This colour is associated with life and how a person relates to life. A person's attitude to life express itself materially, sexually, emotionally, in feelings, intellectually and spiritually. There are many red shades: wine red, dark red, cherry red, strawberry red, orange-red, Buddha red, etc. All shades of red have a special meaning in connection with how a person relates to life and especially how they reflect our individual balance in relation to these attitudes.

When red is experienced in connection with emotional balance in the astral energy field, the colours are quite clean in their expression. The following is dedicated to a description of various shades of red that indicate balance and also of those that indicate a lack of balance.

Royal red
Royal Red is a happy uplifting colour associated with the king's mantle. The colour is associated with a feeling of grandeur and dignity. This red colour contains a bit of blue in it. The high cosmic energies around Christmas time put many people into the feeling of the royal red colour, where appreciation, joy and togetherness with the family are in focus. What we call the true spirit of Christmas is an emotional expression of the royal red colour. When the colour develops further in the direction of higher empathic emotions and the Heart Chakra, called here higher astral emotions / colour, the shade of this red changes to Buddha red.

Pride
Once the feeling of pride is present in a person's astral aura, this is a natural healthy and beneficial pride that may arise in connection with work, personal skills, family, etc.

When there is balance in relation to a feeling of pride, it is associated with respect and appreciation of oneself and other people's values and thus has a good contact with the balanced Solar Plexus Chakra.

Healthy limit-setting anger

When people express their justifiable anger and indignation, there is an almost luminescent neon red fiery shade present in the astral energy field. It is an expression of an emotional system that is flexible and bendy. Anger does not congeal into a convulsive suppressed burst of anger. It comes promptly and directly. It is the healthy, limit-setting anger which is a necessary balancing factor in life, if the individual is to be able to manifest him or herself in life's demanding situations.

When anger is repressed due to unconscious fear, the healthy neon red anger impulse is mixed with black colour, which relates to unconsciousness and suffering and a dark red shade that stresses suffering occurs. It is very important to have good contact with your own natural limit-setting anger. If anger is automatically suppressed, you should try to find the cause of it.

Arrogance

When a person's feeling of pride does not have a balanced contact with the Solar Plexus Chakra, the person cannot respect and appreciate him or herself nor others. Natural pride is thus degraded to inferiority, non-appreciation of oneself and others and it often creates a fertile ground for an emotional driving force, where the unconscious emotional motif is manifested in self-assertion, an excessive need to be seen and confirmed by other people, psychological inflation and arrogance – as such degradation of pride can create a good ground for arrogance. Therefore, in connection with pride it is often said: "pride comes before a fall". People with this unacknowledged emotion may have a difficult life before they begin to recognise their own negative attitudes. These psychological processes of life are often full of suffering. Therefore, the aspect of suffering is also associated with the red colour.

Suffering stressed red

Deep red shades are associated with diverse human processes of suffering. There may be numerous causes of human suffering. A decisive test for all those who find themselves in a process of suffering is whether they keep their dignity and respect for themselves and others. When people suffer, they can be very selfish and lose a lot of their humanity. In order to maintain balance in a process of suffering, it is often necessary to involve the religious aspect in life. If a person is successful in this, the religious higher emotions mix with the deep red colour associated with suffering in the astral energy field, creating relief and often healing too.

Orange

Clear orange in its etheric aspects is first and foremost a healing and health colour. In its positive astral aspect, it is the centring of personality, the strong I, the ambitious I, vitality and health and also the colour of movement.

In its negative aspect, it is self-centeredness and selfishness. The exact shade of this colour is hard to describe, but one can imagine the orange colour of the marigold flower.

Vitality, health and centring

When there is motion in the etheric and astral aura, it means that the etheric life energy flows smoothly without any restrictions or moralising.

As described in Chapter 1, it is through the sun's energy that we obtain our life energy.

Orange also refers to a centred and comprehensive person. Zen Buddhism uses the Hara Chakra as a fixed point. A fixed point is a meditative point that consciousness uses as an anchor while it is occupied with other things and aspects.

Colour of the sun

The colour of the sun obviously cannot be described, because it is light. But the atmosphere of earth dyes the sunlight in a certain orange-yellow shade. This colour provides a feeling of vitality and health and creates a specific astral colour, which has been used in the Eastern world for several thousand years.

This special yellow shade (crocus yellow) is seen in healthy people in their mental aura. It indicates that their mental attitudes are healthy and vitalizing. This feeling spreads to the astral system and is present there as a feeling of relaxed well-being that is similar to a pleasant feeling like when a person has spent a warm summer day on the beach.

The strong I

This strong orange colour mixed with a little ochre is often seen in people with a strong and robust personality. This robust personality character does not shock nor is brought out of balance easily. Their weakness is a psychological closeness that makes them insensitive to other people's opinions, demands and feelings. Therefore, they may seem more selfish and robotic to their surroundings due to their stability and serenity. This type of person is popular within the business community because of their reliability; they are very good at solving individual tasks. Their weakness is that they have difficulty working in a team.

People with a too open and weak I can use this colour to awaken their inner strength of I.

Ambition

The colour of ambition is a mixture of orange and ochre. Ambitions and goals of people are diverse. The ambition to serve other people and society is built on a healthy basis. People who are highly ambitious may seem repulsive to people with weak ambitions. People with high ambitions must have a strong I in order to implement their goals. Willingness to achieve a goal and also a wish for power characterise these kinds of people. Power gives them the opportunity to pursue their goals and ambitions.

Selfish ambition

Selfish ambition is represented by a mixture of the following colours: orange, black, ochre. When a person's ambition is only to seek benefit for him or herself, the colour is mixed with black (lack of awareness). This kind of ambition will always be struggling, because such ambition only serves its owner. The unconscious (black) is often the reason why it becomes difficult to implement this type of ambition, as it is often of an unacknowledged emotional character and such emotion is often connected with the wish to show or prove something to someone in an arrogant manner.

Yellow

Yellow reflects the balance of the astral field and shows how high a degree of consciousness contact a human being has with his or her own deep emotions. Yellow can both prepare the way for emotional / mental strength and also for intuition and sensitivity.

It is also the colour that shows our intellectual capacity, which is usually a mental issue. But intellectual virtue is based on the astral instinct which is associated with the ability of subjective consciousness to distinguish itself from other objects. This ability is associated with the colour yellow, which therefore integrates this mental capacity into its consciousness vibrating area. The more easily a person is able to separate from another's personality, the more stable is his or her personality on a psychological basis. When this ability is refined through mental processes associated with a deep blue colour, gradually an ability to be able to see themself as a part of the whole develops. It is this very fine intellectual ability which has been the main driving force in the development of our society and culture over the last 300 years.

Strength and general intellect

The colour of strength is similar to the yellow colour of the sun, which is described in relation to orange. The difference between them is that the colour of strength is not as bright as the colour of the sun. When this colour is seen in the astral field, it is often in connection with a deep blue colour that may have an association with religious aspects attached to it but also with mental qualities like concentration and focusing ability. This means that this colour is often seen in people with a well functioning intellect. These people often have an academic education. Therefore, the colour is also called the colour of the general intellect. The general intellectual ability is strongly connected to the left hemisphere, which is the rational, calculating half of the brain. Therefore, a casual contact to the delicate yellow colour of intuition, as described below, is advisable. It enables a feeling-based access to the irrational right hemisphere, which often lies idle in a well developed intellectual ability.

Intuition

The colour of intuition is the colour of a delicate, soft yellow lotus flower. This kind of intuition is associated with the open astral system most children are naturally in touch with. It is not the same kind of intuition that is associated with the blue-violet colour. This delicate yellow form of intuition is associated with the Solar Plexus Chakra and the open astral system and is often seen in adults who are highly sensitive. Many such people are often creative, often active as artists or are clairvoyant. To achieve a greater balance in the astral system, it is advisable to establish contact with the yellow colour of the sun for strength and with the balance yellow colour, too.

Balance yellow

This clear yellow colour can be seen around the heads of people, whose intellect is highly developed, while these people also have good contact with their feelings and intuition. This shade is called balance yellow because the colour is a combination of intuition yellow and the yellow associated with strength and general intellect. When these yellow properties are combined, the resulting colour is a pure bright yellow, which also indicates that this colour reflects balance between intellect and intuition.

The essence of intellectual properties is the crystal clear sharpness of thoughts which also have an intuitive ability to comprehend the function of individual parts in a higher connection and higher wholeness. This crystal clear, intuitive ability is expressed through the balance yellow colour.

People with these characteristics are rare. Their sharp intellect and deep intuitive ability will always work for the benefit of humanity because they crystal clearly understand and feel their own function in the whole as well.

The underdeveloped intellect

This type of colour – a mixture of ochre and the yellow colour of the sun in the mental and astral aura indicates underdeveloped or lower intellectual properties. Here, the ability to see a part's function in the whole is not sufficiently developed.

Higher astral colours

Higher astral colours are an expression of higher emotional states, which are from time to time reflected in the astral energy field when a person has a deep, intense contact with them.

These higher feelings are very invigorating and life affirming. They have a very positive effect on the energy field, creating contacts between different layers of consciousness of the energy field. Modern people often use music to get in touch with emotions and moods. A lot of classical music creates these colours in the energy field.

When these higher feelings are refined and developed, they will eventually become what we call spiritual consciousness qualities. When a person manages to be more or less in permanent contact with these higher feelings and they are deeply anchored in his or her personality, they become a consciousness quality.

Higher astral feelings are preliminary stages of spiritual qualities. I have chosen to describe sixteen higher emotions here.

Sky blue

Higher feelings: Healing, peace and direct spiritual communication through telepathy

Sky blue is a very valuable and healing colour. It is seen in people with true, deep peace of mind. The sky blue consciousness state and its deeper feeling creates a deep peace of mind which in turn spreads in the body and all body cells. Peace is an expression of internal integration between personality and all other lower and higher consciousness layers. There are no inner splits, no inner struggles. Everything on an inner and outer basis works in harmonious coexistence and cooperation. Peace is the key word for this harmonious coexistence and cooperation.

The sky blue higher consciousness quality provides peace giving access to love and awareness. Peace is the inaudible and secret password in all higher communications such as telepathy, consciousness transmission or consciousness blending.

It is a very healing colour vibration that is not to be confused with the light blue colour often associated with suppressed and self-denying feelings and thoughts. These repressed impulses are deposited in the lower body and leg area of humans and are seen as an ice blue shade. This ice blue colour is an expression of strong inner repression and displacement of either sexual, emotional / feeling-like or intellectual thought energy.

Exercise that helps against insomnia: People with insomnia should use the sky blue colour in their mental aura. The exercise is done as follows: Lie on your back. Let your head fall into your pillow – be fully relaxed - let your head fall backward into the pillow. When you are deeply relaxed, visualise a clear sky blue colour in front of your mind's eye and carefully place the colour in the mental aura. Feel the colour with your heart – let go of it. And then sleep well.

Rose

Higher feelings: Unconditional love, compassion, humanitarian work, acceptance / self-acceptance, real deep joy

This particular shade of rose is associated with the outward oriented horizontal heart energy. Therefore, the rose shade quality is very important as a mediator of all higher human emotions as they will always be directly connected with the heart energy. The rose colour will always be involved in situations where people give and share, in all humanitarian work, when compassion is awakened, by acceptance / self-acceptance, love, unconditional love and deep joy.

Usually, the heart energy in human beings is activated all by itself. We cannot control the heart energy as it has its own laws. The only thing that can shut off the outward flow of heart energy is our own innate fear and anxiety of contact with our own heart energy. When the heart energy flows, it is directed into the Heart Chakra and chest area from which it subtly, energetically flows into a person, subject, object or situation where there is a real need for it.

People with a balanced energy system will normally have a rose colour about 30 cm in front of the Heart Chakra in their astral energy system. When we encounter a person with this quality, we will always encounter a sense of friendliness, of being welcomed and accepted. A person with the rose quality will naturally have a need for mediation of human thoughts, healing, love, compassion and acceptance.

The rose colour has an outward horizontal motion from the Heart Chakra and is directly connected to the heart energy. Heart energy is a pure healing energy, therefore, it is very healing, uplifting and liberating. It goes where it is needed, always free, and freely available. The rose colour is very helpful when someone needs more emotional contact with his deeper feelings and spiritual qualities and also very supportive in balancing emotions, expressing and transforming them.

Buddha red

Higher feelings: True deeper individuality

This extraordinary red shade is associated with people who have a good grounding; a good ability to differentiate when confronted with reality. This red colour is observed in the Root Chakra, in the astral and mental aura. When a person begins to give out and share from his or her deepest faith, the heart energy is mixed with the red colour and the shade of Buddha red occurs in the higher astral aura.

This colour is mostly seen in the mental field of a Buddha figure in the Buddhist Tangas and therefore, it is called Buddha red. Buddha red can be seen in the energy field particularly in situations in which people express their deeper individual thoughts and ideas. The colour is good to use if a person wants to achieve greater contact between expression, speech and action and his or her deeper individuality. Buddha red will strongly affect the Throat Chakra - significantly if there are repressed emotions, feelings and thoughts in the energy system, preventing the deeper individuality from being expressed. These suppressive mechanisms are mostly related to the three lower chakras. This colour can be used to get these suppressive mechanisms into consciousness.

The colour is also good to use if a person cannot find his or her way in life, cannot find the shelf which they belong to, lacks what is called direction in life. It can provide peace in connection to earth, grounding; it gives a feeling of a quieter, deeper and more stable life direction.

It is a colour to be used with care because it is very active and can create stress. It can create strong reactions in both the Pineal Chakra and the Throat Chakra, especially if the three lower chakras are not balanced.

Red-Purple

Higher feelings: Assertiveness, creatively invigorating, creates emotional tranquillity in groups

This higher astral colour is often seen in people with great self-assertion and originality that borders on geniality, where simplicity is the key word – those are people who have an open contact with a higher consciousness and higher state of love.

The red-purple quality of consciousness often follows a shaman, medicine man, artist, scientist, inventor, and the like.

This colour is very useful in emergency situations, it can absorb and sooth excessive concern and anxiety. For people with auric vision, this colour (state of consciousness) can provide clarification in relation to how a situation develops, or how a developing process ends, so that they can give advice to someone according to the information they gain through their contact with this colour. This colour is also useful in group settings, where it creates a mental sense of community and facilitates peace in the emotional, provides inspiration and supports creativity. Red-purple has the ability to work in several dimensions at once, since it pervades all other colours and dimensions of consciousness with its very rapid vibration. This colour creates a good connection between the Root, Heart and Crown Chakra and therefore a natural polarity between the physical and spiritual reality of a person.

Burgundy (deep magenta)

Higher feelings: Relief and healing of pain, perspective in suffering, dissolution of negative bonds

Taking a wine bottle and holding it up against sunlight is one way to acheive almost the same idea of the colour of this higher astral shade. When consciousness binds itself onto something, which it is not, it creates suffering. The burgundy colour is good at dissolving disease-bearing bonds. This colour may immediately lead consciousness to some other place where it can see suffering from a higher perspective while it can also hide the pain. Through this the painful astral aspect is connected with the higher conscious aspect and burgundy or a related colour occurs in the higher astral aura.

Honey colour

Higher feelings: Inner spiritual leadership, patience, spiritual joy, spiritual humour.

Imagine looking into a honey jar with fresh liquid honey. It is the best way to illustrate this colour. People with this colour in their higher astral aura are very uncommunicative and do little by themselves as measured by the normal personality horizon. Therefore, these people are working in extreme silence and unnoticed in this world because they do not seek any external confirmation or worldly fame. These rare people are often seen around a real and true spiritual teacher or guru or within a nun or monk order of the many spiritual communities worldwide.

This colour is an expression of a personality that at all times humbly submits to its internal and external advisor's will. The ability to submit yourself to the spiritual will and impulse, think and act according to it and bring all this in harmony, is the highest expression and consciousness quality of this colour. It creates a rare inner spiritual joy and humour which these people radiate in a way that is very dry and very down-to-earth - the same perpetual joy and humour with which a person can meet a few very old and mentally fresh people.

Patience is also one of the higher feelings related to this colour. It may be good to use the honey colour where there is a great emotional disguise of a man's higher will, especially where there is envy and jealousy, fear of losing, fear of letting go, and especially in the case of great impatience.

Green colour of natural science (higher mental green)

Higher feelings: Goal orientation - precision - self-discipline

This green consciousness quality can often be seen in people who have the ability to be focussed, precise and self-disciplined. High ethics related to scientific approach is a feature of this attribute. A person's ability to be goal oriented, focused and precise through self-discipline requires high morals and ethics. The ability to work precisely and to be focused exclusively on one goal in order to reach a result or conclusion is often a year-long or life-long challenge for most people. If a goal has to be waited for year after year, for most people it becomes more and more blurred.

This is not the case in people with the higher sense. They reach depths that are often only accessible by people similar to them, to their qualities. Often these kinds of people are known as geniuses, just because they are able to reach so incredibly deep. It is through the ability of precision and dedication that many of humanity's great discoveries have been made and have changed the world and human conditions for the better. Once this ability is used by various governments and regimes where fear is the underlying motif, this outstanding humanitarian ability is, unfortunately, exploited, even destructively.

Balance Green

Higher feelings: Balance and harmony

A man with a balanced chakra and energy system is more or less connected with this higher feeling. Since balance is the key word for all human growth on all levels, this colour quality also has a key position in relation to all other levels of awareness or consciousness of the energy field. The word balance is to be understood as cooperation of various states of consciousness in harmonious accordance and equality.

When there is balance in the Heart Chakra, the rose colour naturally occurs in the astral energy field approximately 30 cm in front of the Heart Chakra. The consciousness quality of balance green provides balance in the chakra system, while the rose colour quality ensures that this balance is given and shared in an equally divided manner. If there is an imbalance of the chakra system, the thought "cast not your pearls before swine" is precise here because the opposite approach leads to an imbalance in the way of sharing and giving yourself. There is no reason to share or give something of great inner values if you would only want to use it for your own profit without deeper ethics. People with these emotional motifs will never be able to appreciate what is shared with them.

Transformation green

Higher feelings: Brings consciousness beyond fear – creates transformation of emotions

This delicate green colour is seen in the energy field of people who are able to bring their awareness beyond fear. The opposite pole of this awareness is fear and anxiety in people who are in connection with the lower astral aura and the Solar Plexus Chakra. Fear and anxiety have a constricting effect on the entire human aura, whereas love and warm feelings have a broadening impact on the energy field. Fear can be overcome by a person learning to relate to it and confronting his or her fears in a constructive way. The consciousness quality associated with this green colour can strengthen and help people to confront their fears on a deeper level. Through exercise they can bring their consciousness beyond fear.

Bringing consciousness beyond fear and anxiety is not something a person succeeds in doing immediately. It requires patience and practice. At first, the person is observing the transformation green and then tries to experience it through feelings. This approach enables bringing this extraordinary feeling to life when fear is experienced. Fear is an irrational emotion that is aurically related to the physical body and to the astral and lower mental aura. The connection between thought, emotion and body can actually be experienced by using specific meditative exercises in which the transformation green colour is used.

Turquoise

Higher feelings: Honesty

The basic quality of the turquoise colour is honesty. Turquoise is a very healing colour that can be very useful in problems in the chakra system and in childhood. People who are honest and do not hide anything from themselves and others have an easy access to this colour and to its consciousness state. If we are afraid to express what we feel, what we basically think and believe, we are closed off from this turquoise consciousness state. The reason why we are afraid to express ourselves and prefer to keep silent is fear of what can happen if we do so freely. As children, very soon we learned to suppress those aspects that were not popular with our parents and surroundings. We learn to adapt to set standards.

From my own personal development viewpoint, turquoise is one of the best colours to work with for these types of childhood experiences that inevitably create problems in the chakra system. Turquoise can indeed create healing in one or more of the chakras, where problems occur.

One of the most natural places to make contact with the turquoise colour is through our nightly dreams. Dreams of a person with chakra problems related to childhood will always in a compensatory way try to redress this imbalance by being as honest as possible.

Light turquoise

Higher feelings: heart contact – the inner child – innocence

Light turquoise in the spiritual aura shows a person's degree of emotional contact with himself or herself. This special form of contact is called the heart contact (feeling contact). A person who has this form of contact with him or herself will also have it with others.

We are all born with heart contact. When the child begins to focus its consciousness on its hands or legs, this means it is slowly beginning to develop an awareness of its body. When the child is about half a year old, it is able to focus its consciousness on other people, which most people who have had contact with small children have experienced. If a person is just a little sensitive, they will certainly realise that there's something special happening when the child focuses its consciousness on others. Most people experience deep joy that is beautiful and uplifting. Some extremely sensitive people may be surprised or even alarmed, that they cannot hide their emotional state from a child.

The child has full heart contact with itself and this heart contact is not yet separated from its inner unity consciousness. Thus, when the child focuses its sight on one thing or person, it does not experience any difference between its subjective consciousness and the object on which its consciousness is focused. Through the heart contact in its focused vision, it experiences a natural unity with the surroundings as it still has not learned, as far as consciousness is concerned, to separate itself from it. Without reservation and with full acceptance it experiences what condition a person is in - whether that person is happy, joyful, sad, disappointed, angry or frustrated. The child senses it all very deeply and without judging. The child observes with complete neutrality. The child, however, can be alarmed when suddenly meeting an adult person with a strong anxiety-stressed defence mechanism when it focuses on that person. In these situations, the child may suddenly start to cry.

The colour of a child's consciousness vibration, in this form of its focusing, is light turquoise which is also an expression of purity of its heart and heart contact with itself and with all. This kind of pure heart contact fades with time as the child grows older. Finally, the child separates from this heart contact so it can become aware of its own feelings, mental resources and the language. This may split the innate ability it originally had. People who are familiar with (and not frightened of) their sensitivity, have the opportunity to restore this ability later in their adulthood.

This colour vibration quality is also connected with honesty, pure heart and innocence. It is through the vibration of honesty and innocence that a human being meets his or her inner child. This colour is beneficial if a person needs to have better emotional contact with their inner child and to provide a better expression to their own inner child's feelings.

Deep blue / blue-violet colours and religious feelings

Higher feelings: true religious belief, the religious aspect

People have always had a real and true need to believe in something mightier and what is beyond physical life. This true human need is reflected in all world religions. A person's religious commitment is reflected in the higher astral aura as a deep blue colour.

Today, the need to believe in something higher is greater than ever. Scientists who specialise in religions speak of a religious wave. The diversity of faiths in the form of religions, philosophies, natural science, spiritual science, gurus, spiritual teachers, and spiritual lifestyles has never been greater than it is nowadays.

The only thing they all have in common is the concept of "faith" and the religious feeling a human being is experiencing. From time to time, faith and religious feeling create blue and blue-violet shades in the higher astral aura.

There are a number of blue, dark blue and violet blue shades which account for some specific higher feelings. What is common to all these shades of blue is their religious theme.

Virgin Mary blue

Higher feelings: religious devotion, healing, music, telepathy, forgiveness, balance between brain hemispheres, concentration, focus.

In its religious meaning and in its feminine aspect, it is the colour of devotion associated with the Virgin Mary. When people achieve mental balance through the use of the left and right hemisphere in the process of their spiritual growth, there is susceptibility towards a higher spiritual impulse in their mental system. This spiritual impulse is the Christ impulse. The aspect of Mary is the divine feminine, nurturing and devoting aspect in a development towards the Christ impulse.

Mental calmness and fully clear goal-orientation are the masculine strengths that are necessary in order to achieve the set goal. The colour quality in its masculine aspect is a very intense deep sense of mental calmness and clarity. Due to a cool overview and also the ability to concentrate and focus, it is, therefore, also called the royal blue colour and the mentioned abilities are natural to some people and they become associated with them. They have leadership features as a natural quality of their personality.

It is the colour that also establishes balance between the two hemispheres and brings the ability of abstract and intuitive thinking into consciousness as it connects and creates a whole, rather than to divide and separate. This colour has a special connection to balance yellow. It also activates the ability of acceptance and forgiveness, and it can have a strong influence on both the Throat Chakra and the Pineal Chakra, where it can even cause strong reactions. Excessive activity in both the Throat Chakra and the

Pineal Chakra should always be noted with care and you should be extraordinarily careful about it. This applies especially to people with clairvoyant abilities, as over-activity, for example, of the Throat Chakra for more than 14 days can create a good ground for Graves' disease and struma. Activity in both the Throat Chakra and the Pineal Chakra, however, usually happens in association with spiritual growth in these chakras but you should always be careful in case of prolonged hyperactivity in these areas.

If so, you should stop all the external and internal activities that contribute to such hyperactivity. For example, a person might tend to use his or her Pineal Chakra excessively in connection with clairvoyance.

Initiation blue

Higher feelings: experience of initiation, religious / spiritual call

It is the colour of a call that will appear in the energy field when a person is initiated from the inside to a spiritual evolutionary process in which this person's call or mission in life is contained. Therefore, this specific blue colour is called initiation blue.

When such inner spiritual initiation takes place, it usually extends over several lives and incarnations with more initiation events. The first initiation event is associated with the initiation blue colour. The very first initiation event is an inflow of spiritual energy into the personality which is filled with intense higher consciousness energy for a short time or for a moment. This energy contains inspiration for the future form and development in the direction of a person's specific call or mission.

The first initiation event can occur in an initiation dream, during meditation, experience of being close to death, and the like. From an inner urge and need, the affected person begins to seek environments where it can develop towards his or her target and call, though at that time the person does not necessarily need to be completely aware of it. This whole development process is guided by the consciousness state of the initiation blue deep in the person's consciousness and heart, where it sits as a Gnostic splinter working on the person year after year.

The initiation blue colour quality is seen in people who have the ability to follow and stick to their inner call, mission and beliefs, although this belief can seem mysterious and unreal in relation to physical reality. Individuals who have experienced a real initiation event ought to follow their belief since they either get sick or die spiritually if they do not do so. This colour is associated with a person's higher consciousness.

Violet

Higher feelings: dignity, grandeur

The spiritual violet colour quality has the highest penetrating radiation. It permeates all other underlying consciousness layers of the energy field and is associated with clear vision and intuition and the higher layers of consciousness.

People with this superior feeling and colour in the energy field, present in a room with others, can become, without any intention, the centre of attention, even if they do not say a word. These people permeate, consciously or unconsciously, though their charisma and presence, the sense of community in a group or gathering of people. They will automatically become the common denominator, spokesmen / spokeswomen of corporate energy.

The violet colour tends to create wholeness and is also associated with the Crown Chakra, which is of course a common energy centre for all of the underlying chakras. The violet colour quality will always be in service for the overall psychological whole and bring people into a higher sense of community of dignity and grandeur.

The earliest records and descriptions of the violet colour found in world literature can be found from times around the birth of Christ. Before that time, according to anthroposophy, it had not been described anywhere. We can, of course, wonder about this, but if we think of colours as different levels of consciousness with different properties and qualities, it is possible that people first had been able to perceive the violet colour vibration only in times around Christ's birth.

Light violet

Higher feelings: divine grace, spiritual alertness, spiritual midwife

This very high, transparent feeling impulse is associated with the internal advisor's level and with higher consciousness, where it is often female wisdom figures that wear and radiate this colour. The colour is a pure spiritual impulse that finds expression in, for example, divine grace, clear intuitions and visions, when it expresses itself in the higher astral aura.

This light violet colour is always present in all consciousness transitions or during any type of higher consciousness shift. A shift in consciousness is present in all people on a daily basis, for example, between wake state and sleep, between dream and reality, between meditation and physical activity. If a person can train his or her consciousness to remain conscious in these transitions, such a person will connect with the light violet colour. In great shifts in consciousness and transitions that occur between birth and death, light violet shades are often seen behind a person and that means a psychological help in these major transitions. Therefore, this colour is called spiritual midwife. To general consciousness, it provides a feeling of divine mercy.

Chapter 4
The Exercises

I have chosen to describe a few simple meditative exercises here that everyone can do. All the exercises will, however, be performed at your own risk. It is not recommened that unbalanced people and the mentally ill do the following exercises.

Practicing exercises of a meditative nature associated with various points of the energy field, has the objective to bring the practicing person into a greater harmony with himself or herself and, thereby, enhance the quality of consciousness in daily life. These exercises will only have an effect if they are practiced regularly. When the exercises are done at regular intervals, it provides a better basis for the energy to flow more effectively in the energy field because relevant points are activated by consciousness. This means that in our daily lives we will be able to function much better mentally and physically. Therefore, I recommend that people who want to practice the following exercises could arrange and perform their own daily exercise schedule of about 15 to 30 minutes. In this way, the maximum effect of these exercises can be achieved.

If you are unsure of how to compose your programme, you are welcome to contact us at **mail@auric-energyfields.com** or you are warmly welcome to join one of our many courses.

For more information, please visit our website at **www.auric-energyfields.com**

I wish you all many pleasant and stimulating hours with the exercises.

Breathing exercises

There are many different exercises in which breathing is included as the focus point for awareness. They all serve the purpose of creating a better connection between, for example, head and body, between thoughts and feelings, between introversion and extroversion, between two energy points, etc. At the same time, they create a better etheric energy flow throughout the whole etheric energy system because breathing is the biggest etheric intake of etheric energy that we humans have available right after the food we eat. For many thousands of years, this fact has been known in the Eastern world. Many people practice the so called "Pranajamas" on a daily basis there. 'Prana' means etheric energy. 'Jama' is the word for breathing exercises.

Breathing exercise between the Pineal Chakra and the Hara Chakra

The exercise is done 10 minutes daily

The purpose of this exercise is to create a natural control over emotions such as excessive anxiety, uncontrollable and overly strong and often camouflaged needs, stubbornness, bossiness, hardheadedness, inflexible attitudes, inadequate power struggles, effort fixation. The breathing exercise between the Pineal Chakra and the Hara Chakra is a basic exercise for a more efficiently functioning energy system, if a person is affected by some of the above-mentioned symptoms. By doing this exercise every day, an energetic connection between the Pineal Chakra and the Hara Chakra, which resembles a bow in the energy field between these two chakras, will be established. The same bow can be observed in people who naturally have this natural control balance.

It is important to mention that while performing a breathing exercise, breathing should be effortless, quiet and deep and should have the same repetitive rhythm pattern during 10 minutes.

Exercise:
1. While inhaling, focus your attention on the Pineal Chakra in the middle of your forehead. Next, focus your attention during inhalation down to the Hara Chakra in the middle of your belly.
2. While exhaling, the attention is focused on the exhaling movement from the Hara Chakra on the centre line up and back to the Pineal Chakra.

Breathing exercise: Hara Chakra – Heart Chakra

This exercise is done regularly, approximately three times a week for 10 minutes

This breathing exercise will increase the energetic exchange between sexuality and love energy that is necessary if you want to achieve a true, more intimate and deeper sexuality.

This exercise is different for men and women, because energies flow differently in men and women.

Men: male respiratory circulation between the Heart and Hara Chakra

1. Inhalation in the Heart Chakra should be led gently down to the Hara Chakra along with attention focused on this area.
2. Exhalation from the Hara Chakra together with attention is led in a bow in the energy field and up to the Heart Chakra.

Women: female respiratory circulation between the Hara and Heart Chakra

1. Inhalation in the Hara Chakra should be led gently, along with attention focussed up to the Heart Chakra.
2. Exhalation from the Heart Chakra together with attention focused on the energy field is led down in a bow back down to the Hara Chakra.

Breathing exercise: the Hara Chakra – the Pineal Chakra

This exercise will involve consciousness and the spiritual together with the sexual and the spontaneous. The exercise is again performed differently in men and women.

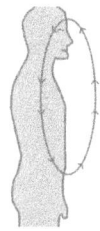

Men: male respiratory circulation between the Pineal Chakra and the Hara Chakra

1. nhalation in the Pineal Chakra in the middle of your forehead should be led quietly down to the Hara Chakra.
2. Exhalation from the Hara Chakra is led in an upward bow back into the energy field to the Pineal Chakra.

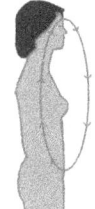

Women: female respiratory circulation between the Hara Chakra and the Pineal Chakra

1. Inhalation is quietly led from the Hara Chakra through the body upwards to the Pineal Chakra.
2. Exhalation from the Pineal Chakra is led into the energy field and in a downward-oriented bow back to the Hara Chakra.

Exercise with a partner

Male/female partner exercise for respiratory circulation between the Hara and the Heart Chakra

5 minutes daily

Stand or sit facing each other with the fronts of your bodies opposite each other - or the woman might lay on top of the man.

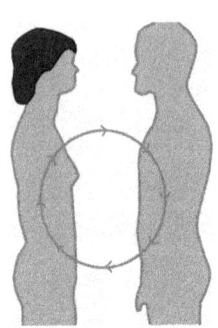

Man: Imagine inhalation to be going out from the Heart Chakra of your female partner. Lead it from there into your own Heart Chakra and further to the Hara Chakra. Exhalation is done from your Hara Chakra into the Hara Chakra of the female partner, through the body of your partner upwards to her Heart Chakra.

Woman: Imagine inhalation to be going out from the Hara Chakra of your male partner. Lead it from there into your own Hara Chakra and further up to your Heart Chakra. Exhalation is done from your Heart Chakra into the Heart Chakra of the male partner, through the body of your partner downwards to his Hara Chakra.

Male/female partner exercise for respiratory circulation between the Pineal Chakra and the Hara Chakra

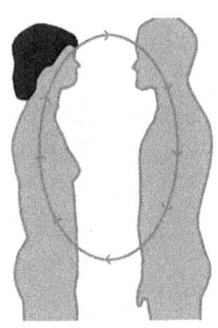

Man: Man: Imagine inhalation to be going out from the Pineal Chakra of your female partner, from there it continues to your own Pineal Chakra and then through the body down to your Hara Chakra. Exhalation is done from the Hara Chakra to the Hara Chakra of your female partner and through her body upwards to her Pineal Chakra.

Woman: Imagine inhalation to be going out from the Hara Chakra of your male partner, from there it continues to your own Hara Chakra and then through the body up to your Pineal Chakra. Exhalation is done from the Pineal Chakra to the Pineal Chakra of your male partner and through his body downwards to his Hara Chakra where the exhalation ends.

Grounding - grounding exercise

5 minutes daily

This exercise creates clarity of mind, while it increases awareness of what is realistically possible and useful in relation to the physical reality. Therefore, this exercise is very important to practice because it brings us in harmony with the physical reality. The exercise is done in slow, gliding, dancing movements, while attention is focused on the points and performed movements.

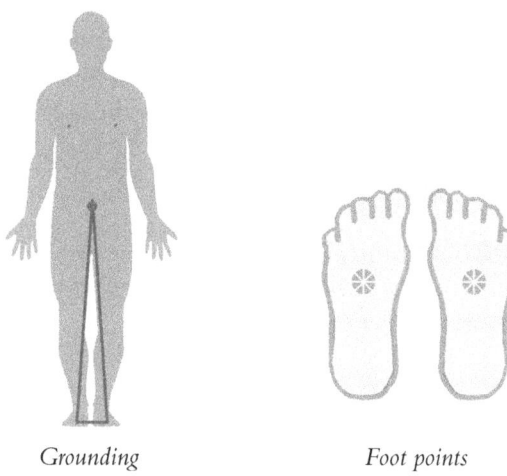

Grounding   *Foot points*

1. Focus your attention on the Hara Chakra (1 - 4 cm below the navel) and create a good contact with that point.
2. Put the weight of your body onto the right foot while you focus your attention on your right foot point.
3. Now place your body weight onto the left foot while you focus your attention on the left foot point.
4. Now bring the body weight back into the centre position while you focus your attention on the Hara Chakra. Then repeat the exercise. You finish this exercise in the Hara Chakra.

Colour visualisation exercise

15 minutes, 3 times a week

1. Visualise a clear red colour. Feel this colour. Place it carefully in the Root Chakra and hold your concentration and the red colour in the Root Chakra for two minutes.
2. This procedure is repeated in each of the above lying chakras. In the Hara Chakra, you visualise a clear orange colour, in the Solar Plexus Chakra a clear yellow colour, in the Heart Chakra a clear green colour, in the Throat Chakra a clear blue colour, in the Pineal Chakra a clear indigo colour, in the Crown Chakra a clear violet colour.
3. When you finish in the Crown Chakra, focus your attention briefly on your Pineal Chakra, Throat, Heart, Solar Plexus, Hara and Root Chakra, each with their respective colours.

The exercise ends when you reach the Root Chakra again.

Colours and exercise

If you are not sure about the colours of the chakras, you can see the colours at www.auric-energyfields.com

Purpose

The exercise will stabilise the natural rotation speed and pulsation of the chakras while it also maintains a healthy state in the chakras. The purpose of this exercise is to bring the various chakras back to their natural state, which for most people will only be experienced as physical and psychical wellbeing. If there are blockages and imbalance in a chakra, a chakra colour will work to eliminate this imbalance while bringing the unconscious psychic material to consciousness.

Difficulties with this exercise:

If there is a blockage in a chakra, you will find it more difficult to keep the concentration in the affected chakra. If you slip out of your concentration, do not worry about it. When you realise your concentration is slipping away, return to the point or chakra where you lost your concentration and continue from there. Should you feel any discomfort during this exercise, stop doing it. If you still want to continue working with your chakras, you should find a person who is aware of how to work with chakras.

Colour meditation with the three synchronous colours

This exercise is done sitting relaxed on a chair or cross-legged. If you want to establish a better contact with your own inner guide, vibration speed in the astral energy field must be higher. To achieve this I can recommend a very soft meditative exercise of colour visualisation. The exercise was created by Bob Moore, and it is one of the exercises that I have personally used with great pleasure and success. Therefore, I would like to share it with all who are interested. To have a better idea of the colours that are used with this exercise, please have a look at them on www.auric-energyfields.com

People who use this exercise should know that it will bring all psychological material into consciousness and is the reason a person cannot understand or listen to his or her inner wisdom. This psychological material is to be processed and recognised if the exercise is to be helpful. People who have psychic problems or suffer from some psychic imbalance should not do this exercise. Let me remind the readers that the exercises are done at their own risk.

If this meditative colour exercise is done carefully once a day for about 10 minutes for half a year, the inner wisdom will be attracted to the higher vibration frequency in the astral energy field. Human consciousness is a wonderful tool to use when it comes to colours. By visualising the colour and placing it carefully in the energy field, it can be observed there for up to 48 hours.

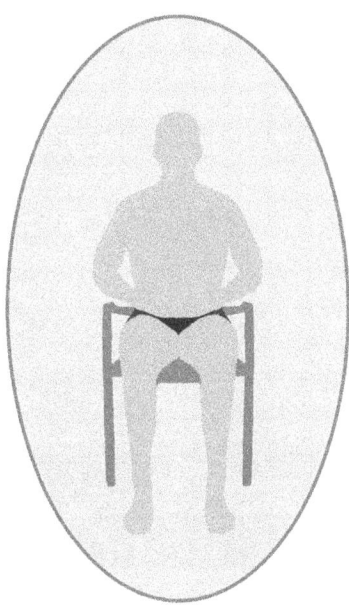

A person works with three specific colours. The golden colour, rose and sky blue. For one week, a the person works with gold, the following week with rose and then the other week with sky blue.

Exercise

1. Imagine the colour in front of your inner eye. When you have a good contact with this colour, feel it with your heart.
2. Place the colour in the essence point 30 cm above your head and let it slide down on all sides, on the front and back part of your body, of a distance of approximately 30 cm from the body to a point 30 cm under your feet.
   Do it carefully and give yourself plenty of time.
3. Visualise light in the point under your feet (only pure light, with no colour, nor white light). Pull the light up from between your feet - further up between your legs – then up through the inner of your body, neck and head - up to the point 30 cm above your head. Let the light loose and sit in silence for a moment.
   This is the end of the exercise.

Honey colour

5 minutes, 3 times a week

This colour visualisation exercise is good to use when there is a lot of emotional concealment of a person's higher will. Especially when this emotional concealment has some connection with envy and jealousy, fear of losing and fear of letting go. It can also be used if a person suffers from a excessive impatience.

1. For a moment direct your attention to the Heart Chakra, Throat Chakra, the Pineal Chakra and the Crown Chakra.
2. Then direct it to the point 30 cm above your head, at the top of the mental aura and visualise the honey colour and place it in that point.
3. Let the colour spread around the head and the whole mental aura, so that it eventually covers the entire mental aura. End the visualisation of this colour in the Heart Chakra at the base of the mental aura.
4. Let the colour loose and direct your attention for a moment to the Hara Chakra, Root Chakra, and your feet.

Special exercises

Exercises to help prevent insomnia
Many people suffer from insomnia. The reasons might be diverse, but a common feature is the feeling of unrest in the mind and body. By imitating the condition of the energy field when we have peace of mind and body, we can achieve a natural contact with our own deeper peace.

Deeper peace radiates as a sky blue shade in the energy field, especially in the mental aura. You might have a look at this shade of blue on **www..auric-energyfields.com**.

The exercise is done during the phase of falling asleep, but it can naturally be made any time we want to be in touch with our own deeper peace. Put your pillow in a position so you can fully relax your head, neck and shoulders when you lie down.

1. Lie on your back.
2. Let your head fall into the pillow – allow yourself to be fully relaxed. Let your head fall, fall, fall.
3. When you are deeply relaxed, visualise sky blue colour in front of your mind's eye, feel the colour and place it carefully in the whole mental aura - over the head, on the front, right and left side and back part, on the upper back, shoulders, chest area. Let the colour loose and sleep well.

Cleansing of space and aura
Cleansing and transforming energy in a room with a bad atmosphere is done through the four cardinal directions. Here is a description of how it is done.

1. Stand in the middle of the room facing the corner that is closest to north. Imagine that through a deep breath you inhale all the bad energy from the north corner and visualise black colour. During exhalation, you visualise white light breathing out in the direction of the north corner.
2. Then turn right, facing the east corner. There you repeat the same action with breathing and visualisation as you did in the north corner.
3. Turn right towards the south corner and repeat the very same action.
4. Turn right, facing the west corner and repeat the same action again.

Then the room is cleansed of bad energy and this process is complete. A person can possibly even cleanse his or her aura afterwards. This is done in a standing position by visualising light in the point 30 cm above the head and letting the light fill all the areas of the energy field. The person starts at the top and finishes down at a point approximately 30 cm below the feet.

Then the exercise is finished. If the person has had body contact with others throughout the day, they can cleanse his or her aura by taking a shower for at least five minutes. Also, other techniques of how to cleanse a person's aura are presented on our courses.

Waste Energy - healing exercise with a partner - 2 times a week

The energy that is wasted or lost is the energy that accumulates on the upper part of the back, where it creates problems in and around this body area. These problems can manifest themselves as a headache, sharp pain in the teeth, tension and stiff muscles in the shoulder and neck, a flicker in front of the eyes. In order to eliminate these symptoms, the following healing exercises have been created by Bob Moore. For more information, you might like to read about the waste energy point that is located on the upper part of the back in Chapter 1, the important etheric points.

Important: Approximately 24 hours should pass before the recipient of this healing exercise can provide the same healing to the partner who provided this healing.

Stand on your partner's left side. Place the palm of your left hand on the forehead of your partner and place your right hand on your partner's back part of head.

Keep your hands in this position for a few minutes. This is done to come into harmony with your partner and also so that he or she can be relaxed.

1. Place the palm of your right hand on the second thoracic vertebra on the back and the palm of your left hand on the spleen point (at the edge of the ribs vertically down from the left nipple, or 7 ribs).
2. Circulate with your right hand in a counterclockwise direction so that your palm is always in direct contact with the second thoracic vertebra.
   Touch this area with even wider oval movements towards the shoulder points on the right and left shoulder edge.
3. When you have reached the shoulder points, start to circulate back to the starting point.
4. When you have reached the starting point, rest the palm of your right hand on the second thoracic vertebra for a moment. This is the end of this exercise.

Overview of points
Front part of the body

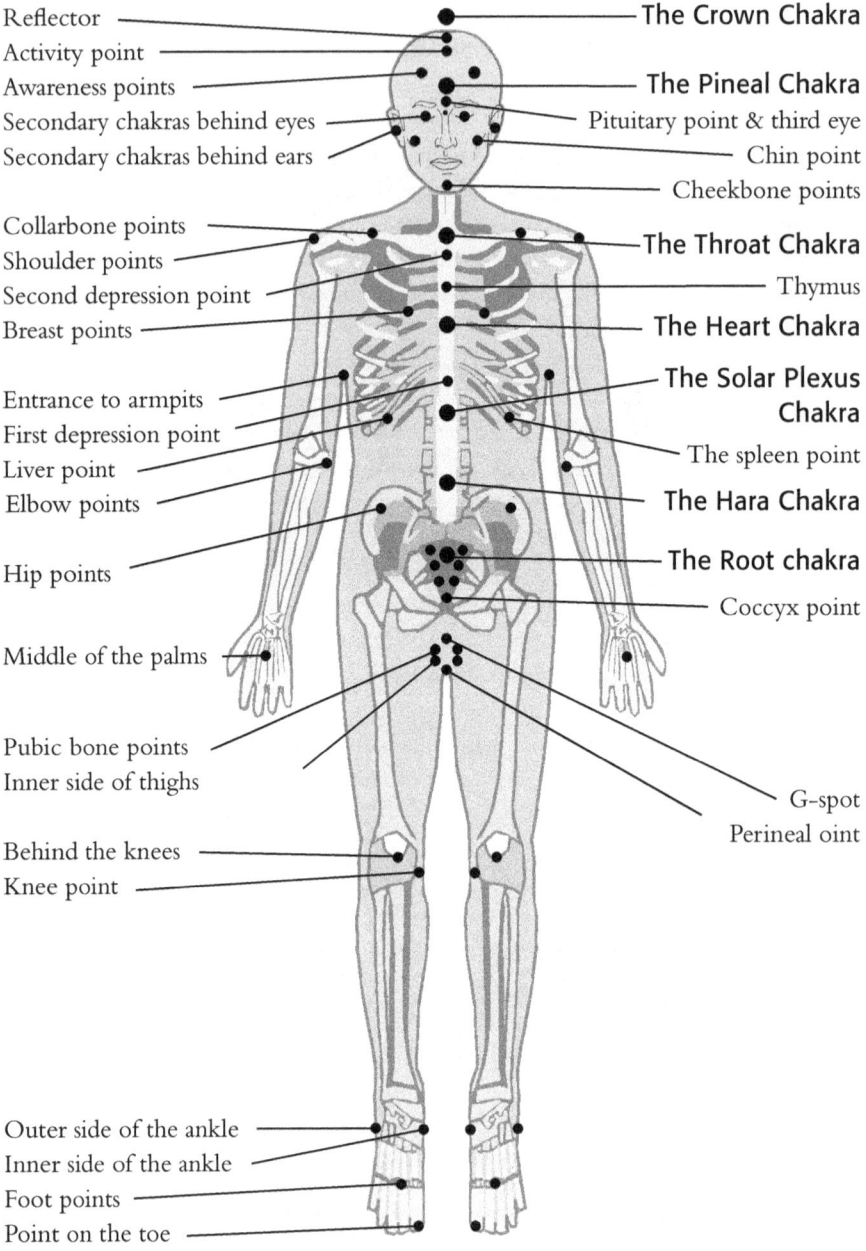

- Reflector
- Activity point
- Awareness points
- Secondary chakras behind eyes
- Secondary chakras behind ears

- The Crown Chakra
- The Pineal Chakra
- Pituitary point & third eye
- Chin point
- Cheekbone points

- Collarbone points
- Shoulder points
- Second depression point
- Breast points

- The Throat Chakra
- Thymus
- The Heart Chakra
- The Solar Plexus Chakra

- Entrance to armpits
- First depression point
- Liver point
- Elbow points

- The spleen point
- The Hara Chakra
- The Root chakra
- Coccyx point

- Hip points
- Middle of the palms

- Pubic bone points
- Inner side of thighs

- G-spot
- Perineal oint

- Behind the knees
- Knee point

- Outer side of the ankle
- Inner side of the ankle
- Foot points
- Point on the toe

Chapter 4 — Exercises

Overview of points
Back part of the body

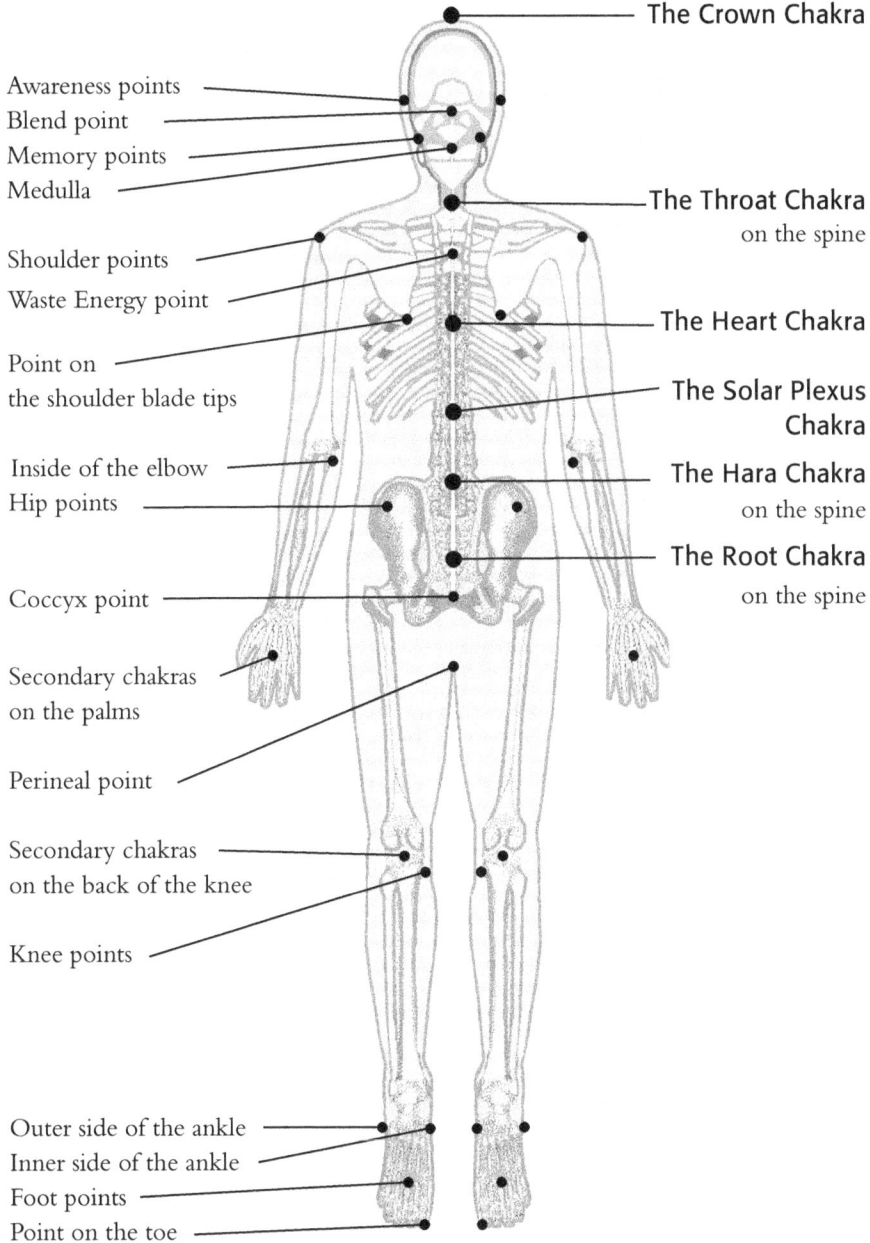

- The Crown Chakra
- Awareness points
- Blend point
- Memory points
- Medulla
- The Throat Chakra
  on the spine
- Shoulder points
- Waste Energy point
- The Heart Chakra
- Point on the shoulder blade tips
- The Solar Plexus Chakra
- Inside of the elbow
- Hip points
- The Hara Chakra
  on the spine
- The Root Chakra
  on the spine
- Coccyx point
- Secondary chakras on the palms
- Perineal point
- Secondary chakras on the back of the knee
- Knee points
- Outer side of the ankle
- Inner side of the ankle
- Foot points
- Point on the toe

Frank Lorentzen (born in 1949) is a musician, composer, healer, clairvoyant and author of books.
He has been providing education based on the content of this book for many years.

Frank Lorentzen grew up in the north of Aarhus, Denmark. Through his clairvoyant access to nature and his obvious musical talent he soon parted ways from his surroundings. At the age of nine, he was fascinated by the wondrous world of music and his fascination resulted in teaching himself to play the piano, the guitar and other musical instruments. He made his living through his musical talent until he was 36 years old.

In 1972 he began to practice meditation on a daily basis. In 1982, this meditative practice resulted in a "mystical experience" which was his initiation to begin work as a healer.

The topic of this book is based on vivid experiences from his childhood and from his adult life. Frank Lorentzen focuses on the whole person and the spiritual consciousness form and how this consciousness form is integrated in personality. In 1983, he met the outstanding Irish healer Bob Moore, who has been a great inspiration and significant support for him.

Since 1985, Frank Lorentzen has been active as a healer and has worked with many individuals and groups too. He works with healing through music, sound, dreams and energy work in the energy field and the body. He has had many concerts, courses and seminars both in his home country and abroad.

Alongside his teaching and individual consultations, he has released nine music CDs at Phoenix Music:

Hands 1986
Centring 1989
Summer Vision 1990
The Balance of Gaia 1994
Alpha 1997

Harmonic Resonance 1999
Serenity 2003
Concert for the Prague Castle 2003
Chakramusic 2007

CDs can be purchased at www.aromanet.dk

Frank Lorentzen
mail@auric-energyfields.com
www.auric-energyfields.com

Music composed, arranged and recorded by Frank Lorentzen
All CDs can be ordered at www.aromanet.dk

Hands   1986
New age classics. The notes of the universe, the music of the spheres. Since 1986, "Hands" has especially been used for healing, meditation and expansion of consciousness. It has sold over 250,000 copies around the world.

Centering   1989
Meditative. Presents an intense and soulful beauty.
Centering has sold over 100,000 copies in Japan and 175,000 around the world.

Summer Vision   1990
Melodic music with flute and electric piano as the main instruments.
Many of the the melodies on Summer Vision have been used as theme songs for various radio programmes in Denmark and around the world because of their atmosphere.
The melodies are inspired by nine archetypes from the present, ancient Greece and Rome.

Music composed, arranged and recorded by Frank Lorentzen

The Balance of Gaia   1994

Both melodic and meditative music which touches the mind and heart. The relationship and co-operation of man with nature, and the genetic intelligence of life through wisdom is the source of inspiration for "The Balance of Gaia". Gaia is the ancient godess of the Earth within Greek mythology. "The Balance of Gaia" has sold 75,000 copies around the world and is used as background music in clinics.

Alpha   1997

Instruments: Quartz crystal singing bowls, Tibetan singing bowls, cymbals, sounds of nature, keyboard. "Alpha" is build around two long piece of music/sound which bring the listener into a state of being between sleep and awake. This state is called the "Alpha state" by brain scientists, and it has a regenerating and stress releasing effect on the mind.
The Alpha state is also the first step within meditation, where in time you can achieve a greater relaxed state of being awake, which is necessary in achieving greater depths in meditation. "Alpha" has sold over 100,000 copies.

Harmonic Resonance   1999

Healing and deeply relaxing. "Harmonic Resonance" works particularly inside the body, which becomes deeply relaxed.
The unique sound of the crystal singing bowls combined with meditative music is a solace for body and soul. Body, mind and spirit become a trinity, which makes "Harmonic Resonance" very healing and regenerating. "Harmonic Resonance" has sold over 150,000 copies.

Serenity 2003

"Serenity" was composed during a week-long stay in connection with a concert at Prague Castle in April, 2003. The music is inspired by the Springtime in the garden of the castle with all its unbelievable amount of Spring flowers. "Serenity" is very uplifting, releasing, beautiful and very tender. "Serenity" brings the listener in contact with their own inner soulful beauty. "Serenity" has sold over 150,000 copies.

Concert for Prague Castle 2003

"Concert for the Prague Castle" is a live concert at Janak Hall in the Prague Castle. The live recording is available on both CD and DVD and is recorded by the best photographers and sound technicians in the Czech Republic. The effects of the live concert on both CD and DVD are very deep and meditative. The impact of the 200 meditating people in the audience is clear on both the CD and DVD. Many people use the CD / DVD as mental hygiene. The effects are cleansing and healing. The live concert has sold over 50,000 copies.

Chakra Music 2007

"Chakra Music" is inspired by many years of dedicated work with the relationship of sound and music to the seven chakras. These experiences have been transferred to "Chakra Music", which has a balancing effect on the chakra system. In addition, there are three chakra meditations which are guided by the sound of seven chakra-tuned crystal singing bowls, and which have a wonderful balancing effect on the chakra system. Since 2007, "Chakra Music" has been on the Top 20 list of best selling CDs at Fønix Music and has sold 65,000 copies.

www.auric-energyfields.com

www.ingramcontent.com/pod-product-compliance
Lightning Source LLC
Chambersburg PA
CBHW031629160426
43196CB00006B/342